To Sherry
Happy Celebration!
Ben Clement

Loved seeing you!

*This creation is dedicated to my beloved husband,
Johnny, whose devotion, love and inspirational support sustain me.*

Beverly Reese Church

Copyright © 2005 by Entertaining Celebrations, L.L.C.
3525 Prytania Street, Suite 230, New Orleans, LA 70115
All rights reserved. No part of this book may be reproduced
without written permission from the publisher.
Photographs copyright © 2005 by Cheryl Gerber and Chris Granger.
Printed in Canada.
ISBN 0-9659817-1-1

SEASONAL CELEBRATIONS

by
Beverly Reese Church

with
Sallye English Irvine

Photographs by
Cheryl Gerber and Chris Granger

Illustrations by
Katie Rafferty

contents

Spring

Easter Breakfast
PAGE 6-9

April in Provence
PAGE 10-13

Flower Power
PAGE 14-17

Graduation Party
PAGE 18-21

Red Hot Rose Soirée
PAGE 22-25

Picnic in the Park
PAGE 26-29

Summer

Family Reunion and Fish Fry
PAGE 32-35

Pool Party
PAGE 36-39

Fourth of July
PAGE 40-43

Caribbean Party
page 44-47

Biking Bash
PAGE 48-51

An Al Fresco Event
PAGE 52-55

Recipes
page 108-155

Index
page 156-160

contents

Autumn

Farmer's Market Dinner
PAGE 58-61

Blowout Barn Party
PAGE 62-65

Girl's Night Out
PAGE 66-69

Posh Polo Party
PAGE 70-73

Wild Game Dinner
PAGE 74-77

Black & White Bash
PAGE 78-81

Winter

Holiday Prgressive Party
PAGE 84-87

House Party
PAGE 88-91

Valentine Dinner
PAGE 92-95

A Moveable Mardi Gras
PAGE 96-99

Milestone Birthday
PAGE 100-103

Gallery Opening Gala
PAGE 104-107

Recipes
page 108-155

Index
page 156-160

Spring

Spring is a celebration of nature. All the world seems a lush, verdant paradise – ablaze in a profusion of perfumed, colorful blossoms. The weather tends to be gloriously sunny with sweeping, delicious breezes. And everything seems brighter and more vibrant. It is a time of splendid renewal — fresh and fun. So, it is a grand time for reveling in the sundry celebrations of spring — Easter, Mother's Day and graduations galore. It is also the ideal occasion for garden gatherings and all sorts of al fresco entertaining. Consider hosting a party on the patio or a festive brunch in the backyard. Delight in the beauty and fragrance of the season.

The Party Plan

Easter morning is a time for togetherness and for rejoicing. It is a terrific time for a family brunch where everyone is involved in the cooking or creating. After an early morning egg hunt, continue the excitement and activity by preparing a sumptuous feast. The adults do the cooking while the children decorate hard-boiled eggs to be used as place cards for the table. Older children lend a helping hand with the smaller set. For an extra touch of fun, the children also get to crown the cake with a heavenly halo of whipped cream and add red, ripe seasonal strawberries.

...r lettuce and bright, spring blooms create ...rful setting for Easter brunch. Living lettuce ... long-lasting, attractive, edible décor. A wooden ...berry basket serves as a clever container for ... pansies and vases brimming with hyacinths, ...ils, tulips and other favorite flowers.

Menu
Commander's Palace
Freshly Squeezed Orange Juice
Brandy Milk Punch*
Eggs Sardou*
Shrimp Cognac and Andouille Stone Ground Grits*
Buttermilk Biscuits with Strawberries and Sweet Cream*
* Recipe in the back of the book.

Flower wreath welcomes guests.

A petite bouquet, placed inside a small jar of water, and a ring of sweet, red strawberries complete the cake.

A cluster of vibrant Gerbera daisies in plush rye grass.

Flair for the Affair
- Make or buy bunny ears for everyone attending.
- Dance the bunny hop.
- Encourage the children to create a play.

Décor and More
- Living lettuce in containers
- Egg place cards
- Wooden box of rye grass with flowers

Invitation Ideas
- Traditional invitation by phone, since this is a casual family party.
- Have the children create Easter themed cards using paints or markers stating "Hop on Over to Our House."
- Deliver small baskets filled with grass and colorful plastic eggs Place the party particulars inside the eggs and add a great big bow.

Hard-boiled eggs are offered as personalized place cards. Each egg is nestled in a moss-laden pot.

How To

Living Lettuce in Containers

Purchase butter lettuce complete with roots and soil. Remove from container and place in a cup or goblet filled with water. Gently and carefully open the lettuce leaves to make the head full and pretty.

Egg Place Cards in Pots

Hard-boil several eggs. When eggs are cool and dry they are ready to decorate. Use permanent markers in a variety of colors to personalize and decorate the eggs.

For the pots, cover the hole in the bottom with cling floral adhesive, then add oasis. Cover the oasis with moss. Put a few flowers in a water pick and insert into the oasis. Add the egg.

Wooden Box of Rye Grass with Flowers

Cover the bottom of a wooden box with heavy black plastic (to prevent water from leaking). Fill the box with multi-purpose soil mix about 1 1/2 inches deep. Sprinkle the soil with water. Spread rye grass seed all over the top of the soil and place the planter in the sunlight. You should have a thick, carpet of green rye grass in about a week. Put Gerbera daisies in water picks and insert into rye grass.

The Party Plan

The inspiration for this sensational, sunflower-strewn soirée comes from one of our favorite books, "A Year in Provence," by Peter Mayle. (So, in lieu of the expected April in Paris we shift southward to celebrate April in Provence.)

Invite 6 to 8 friends (or favorite francophiles) for a warm, wonderful evening of wine and French fare. The dress is casual chic or fashionably French.

For the ultimate ease in entertaining, ask that each couple be in charge of one course – French bistro-style cuisine – and that each bring their favorite wine from France (preferably Provence). Ooo la la!

Menu
Galatoire's
Wines from Provence
Oyster Pan Roast*
Chicken Bonne Femme*
Bread Pudding with Banana Sauce*

Recipe in the back of the book.

The buffet table looks warm and inviting draped with an authentic Provençal cloth and adorned with earthenware. Cache pots are piled with apples and a menu card written in French announces the repast. Red gladiolas, blue delphinium and sunflower pompoms are arranged to be reminiscent of the rows of cypress trees and fields of flowers found in the Provençal countryside.

Pottery from Deruta, Italy

Flair for the Affair

- Greet your guests in French, "Bienvenu en Provence mes amis. Entrez!"
- French music fills the air – Charles Aznavour, Edith Piaf, Paris Combo or your favorite French artist.
- Bundles of herbes de Provence make fun French favors.
- Hold a wine tasting.
- After a few glasses of wine, start a cancan line or learn a French folk dance.

Décor and More

- Sunflower napkin rings
- Painted pots
- Setting up the wine tasting

Invitation Ideas

- A split of French wine tied with a card detailing the party particulars and specifying the course to bring.
- Tie the invitation to a single sunflower with a bright bow.
- Tie a card to a baguette with red, white and blue striped French flag ribbon.

Asparagus spears and branches of fresh rosemary encircle a single sunflower.

A plump packet of herbes de Provence at each place setting makes a festive favor.

Sunflowers appear everywhere – from the tablecloth to the tabletop.

How To

Sunflower Napkin Rings

Purchase grapevine rings at a craft store along with faux sunflowers. Remove the flower from the leaves then hot glue the flower to the grapevine ring. (If you cannot find grapevine rings, use a silk tulip leaf. Form each leaf into a ring and hot glue together.)

Painted Pots

Buy small clay pots (about 4 inches in diameter). Brush the pots with clear polyurethane on the outside only. Let dry. Sponge the pots lightly with white acrylic paint to partially cover while still allowing some of the terracotta color to show. When the paint is dry, sponge lightly with basil-colored acrylic paint. When that paint is dry, spray pots with polyurethane. Let dry. Cover the hole in the bottom of each pot with cling floral adhesive. Fill each pot with water-soaked oasis, add a sunflower to each pot and surround with moss.

Setting up the Wine Tasting

Have each guest bring a bottle of wine. Bag each of the wines and place wine glasses, a notepad or card along with a pen in front of each bottle. After everyone has had a chance to taste and rate the wines on a scale of one to ten, reveal the wines, the ratings and the tasting notes.

Flower Power

The Party Plan

For this fantasy flower fête, invite 6 to 8 best girlfriends. The festivities take place in the garden. The hostess hands each friend a lovely lei upon arrival and then the fun begins. When the gang's all there, take a photograph of the bevy of beauties to be tucked into a flowery frame at the party's end. Start with some creative crafts – paint T-shirts and decorate picture frames – followed by the frosting and eating of cupcakes. Games are played in the garden, including three-legged races, a hula hoop contest and such old-fashioned favorites as "Red light, Green light" and "Mother May I ?" Any remaining energy can easily be expended during dancing to a selection of great "oldies but goodies." For the finale, finish off by making individual pita pizzas embellished with a variety of garden toppings.

Menu
Ford Church-Cottonwood Institute

Cranberry Sparkle*

Organic Peppermint Tea and Apple Juice*

Perfect Pizza Pita Pockets*

Cupcakes

World Famous Organic Banana Bread*

Mississippi Mud Brownies*

Recipe in the back of the book.

Fresh flowers crown the cupcakes.

A petite, pretty box filled with art supplies and all tied up in a bright cloth napkin and ribbon accompanies the invite.

The hostess, be it a birthday girl or not, has a designated daisy-bedecked throne.

Flair for the Affair

- Set up lawn bowling and horseshoes.
- Learn how to make leis.
- Provide chalk for playing hopscotch and creating sidewalk art.

Décor and More

- Flower blanket
- Flower cupcakes
- Flower photo frames

Invitation Ideas

- A bright cloth-tied box along with the party particulars.
- A flower-topped pen tied with invite.
- A flower pot cake with invite.

A fun blanket featuring fabulous faux flowers and colossal dragonflies awaits for relaxing and refueling during and after the activities.

Candle lollipops in clay pots and favor boxes.

Fresh flowers crown the cupcakes.

Whimsical frames are embellished with hearts and flowers.

How To

Flower Blanket
Cut a piece of soft tulle the size of the blanket or cloth to be used. Place the tulle atop waxed paper and hot glue leaves and flowers in desired areas. Carefully peel the waxed paper away from the tulle as you hot glue each leaf and flower. Spread blanket or cloth on the ground and cover with the decorated tulle. Add dragonflies and butterflies (purchased at craft store or discount store).

Cupcakes with Fresh Flowers
Cut clear, plastic straws into 4-inch long lengths. Cut the stems of long-lasting flowers such as pompom daisies or chrysanthemums to just under 4 inches and insert into the straws. Poke the flower straws into the tops of frosted cupcakes.

Flower Photo Frames
Purchase wooden photograph frames and foam cut-outs at the craft store. Simply remove adhesive from cut-outs and stick on frames to decorate.

Candle Lollipops in Clay Pots
Find favorite shaped candles (we used lollipops) and place in painted 4" clay pots. To keep lollipops upright, add styrofoam in the pots to fit, leaving an inch from the top. Fill with M&Ms or Skittles.

Favor Boxes
Take 4" x 4" x 4" white boxes and place a water soaked, mini-deco holder (floral foam on a self-adhesive base). Add button pom poms to cover. Fill boxes with favorite toys (whistles, sidewalk chalk, flashing rings...)

Flower Pot Cake Invite
Boil small clay flower pots in water for 20 minutes. When pots are cool and dry, place a cookie over the hole in the bottom (macaroons work well). Prepare your favorite cupcake or brownie mix and pour into pots. Bake according to the package directions. Meanwhile, cut clear, plastic straws into 3-inch segments and insert a faux silk flower into each straw. Poke a flower straw into each cooled, pot. Tie a cute card detailing the party information onto each stem and hand-deliver.

The Flower Power Girls enjoying a spot of peppermint tea between activities.

17

Graduation Party

The Party Plan

This fun and funky party is fabulous for fêteing your favorite female graduate. Whether she has just graduated from law school, medical school, business school or received another distinguished degree, she's now set to establish her career and ready to really start entertaining. So, gather a dozen or more guests for an outdoor seated lunch. Shower the honoree with glorious gifts she'll need to set up housekeeping — and to launch her on her way as a future hostess — everything from artwork to sensational serving pieces. To ensure heaps of laughter and lively entertainment during the event, arrange to sing karaoke to memorable tunes from the graduate's high school and college years.

Menu
Ralph's on the Park

White Wine
Iced Tea

Jalapeño Shrimp with Spiced Corn Salsa on Tomato Pinwheels*

Lemon Herb Chicken

Lentil, Barley and Rice Salad*

Bete Noire with White Chocolate Drambuie Sauce*

Recipe in the back of the book.

Chargers painted with lively lemon-yellow flowers serve as placemats for the party as well as take-home presents for the honoree. A playful painting is another great gift. (Chargers and painting by artist Karin Rittvo.)

nciful hand-painted umbrella by Josanne rand and tulle-draped table make a vibrant, y setting for lunching outdoors.

A fun flower fly swatter tied with tulle and tucked into a pretty pink kalanchoe plant makes a enchanting invitation.

19

Flair for the Affair

- Set up a karaoke machine.
- Pass out feather boas.
- Whisk everyone away for an afternoon sail following lunch.

Décor and More

- Painted umbrella
- Napkin rings
- Tulle tablecloth
- Flower charger

Invitation Ideas

- Fly swatter invitation in a plant.
- A card featuring a photograph of the honoree as a child, or in cap and gown.
- Roll up invitation like a diploma and tie with tassels.

Set among a myriad of flowers at the honoree's placesetting is the perfect present: a whimsical painting by artist Josanne Sjostrand. The napkin rings are designed to match the chargers.

A gorgeous goblet hand-blown by Teri Walker.

How To

Painted Umbrella

Buy a white canvas umbrella. Thin gesso paint with water (2/3 gesso, 1/3 water). Put down a drop cloth and place the open umbrella low to the ground or in umbrella stand so it is easy to paint. Paint the entire umbrella with gesso and let dry. Then paint the umbrella with a base coat of yellow acrylic paint. Let dry. Draw your design on the umbrella in pencil and then paint, starting at the top, with acrylic paint. After the paint is dry, spray with satin polyurethane to seal.

Tulle Tablecloth

Measure the table you are using to buy enough tulle to cover the top and extend to the floor with two extra feet on each end. Buy the same amount of tulle in three fun colors. (We used red, hot pink and bright blue.) Attach the three pieces together side by side (with loose whip stitches or pins). Spread the tulle over the table allowing it to puddle on each side. Pick up about 10-inches from each end of the tulle and tie loosely with extra tulle in contrasting colors or with ribbon.

Flower Chargers

Buy 14-inch cake rounds at a party supply store. Spray both sides of the round with the color of the flowers you are using. (We used hot pink.) Buy enough silk flowers to allow for 24 to 28 flowers per charger. Hot glue flowers to the charger starting with the perimeter moving toward the center until the charger is full.

Napkin Rings

Cut napkin ring base (as shown in photograph) from gesso backed canvas. Hot glue about six silk leaves to the canvas, then hot glue several flowers to the center. (We used roses and hot pink Gerbera daisies.)

he completed napkin ring and canvas base.

charger blanketed in bright blooms adds a dash of panache.

The Party Plan

Celebrate the annual "Run for the Roses" in spectacular style with a red-hot rose soirée. Invite 20 to 30 guests for a lavish, late lunch scheduled to start about an hour and a half before the Kentucky Derby. Commence the festivities by offering a tray of traditional mint juleps along with ruby-hued libations. Serve lunch buffet-style, then let the "betting" begin. After all the wagers have been placed, guests gather around the television for the big race. Immediately following the finale, everyone retires to the flower-festooned backyard for decadent desserts and rose champagne.

Menu
Brennan's
Rose Champagne
Mint Juleps
Mr. Funk of New Orleans*
Garden Gazpacho*
Trout Nancy with Lemon Butter Sauce*
Brabant Potatoes*
Minted Fresh Fruit Compote
Garlic Bread*
Chocolate Bourbon Balls and a Selection of Sweets
*Recipe in the back of the book.

Rose covered tablecloth.

Rosy libations and a selection of sweets are elegant served upon, and amidst, heirloom silver. Bouquets of white roses at the table's edge are a stunning note in a sea of red petals.

A rose-festooned sash adds an eye-catching accent to the back of a folding chair swathed in striped fabric.

Flair for the Affair

- Request that all guests wear at least a touch of red.
- Ladies should don showy chapeaux, with hats optional for the gentlemen.
- Pass out sheet music for "My Old Kentucky Home" and encourage everyone to sing.
- Circulate betting baskets.

Décor and More

- Rose covered tablecloth
- Rose-adorned umbrella
- Rose chair sashes
- Painted champagne flutes
- The betting process

Invitation Ideas

- A miniature bottle of bourbon tied with a red rose.
- Roll up a racing form with the party details outlined on the other side, tie with a red ribbon and add a red rose.
- A small mint plant with julep recipe and party information.

An opulent cascade of deep red roses, beneath a rose-dappled umbrella, makes a show-stopping tablescape.

A gorgeous garland of roses rims the umbrella.

How To

Rose-Covered Tablecloth

Cut triangles of green cloth. Each triangle is 54" x 54" x 46" (eight panels for a 72-inch round table; five panels for a 60-inch round table). Spread out approximately 60 silk red roses closely and evenly. Hot glue down all the roses. Then hot glue a variety of silk leaves and greenery in, under and around the roses.

Place an inexpensive floor-length cloth on the table as an underlay. (We used a white tablecloth.) Find the center of the cloth and snip a small hole for the umbrella to go through. Put umbrella into the table. Place the rose-covered triangle panels on the table with the top point at the umbrella pole. Pin the panels together with several large hat pins so that they slightly overlap. Wrap a red or green ribbon around the base of the umbrella pole catching the tips of all the panels and tie the ribbon tightly to hold.

Rose Chair Sashes

Cut sashes out of green fabric (45" x 7"). Hot glue the edges of the sash, turning under about 1/2-inch. Hot glue greenery and several roses along sash. Drape fabric around chair and secure by wrapping sash around the back and pinning.

Rose-Adorned Umbrella

Pin sashes with roses and greenery along the perimeter of the umbrella. Use two sashes to wrap the umbrella pole. Pin or hot glue red roses at top and on the umbrella.

Champagne flutes hand-painted with roses make memorable, marvelous favors.

Painted Champagne Flutes

Wash the glasses and let them dry without touching them. Then paint the glasses or apply tranfers. (We used Paint 'n' Press transfers made by Delta.) You may also paint designs freehand using paint designed to be used on glass or tile. Finish by applying a clear, water-based topcoat. (Some glass paint requires baking, follow the directions on the paint that you choose.)

Betting Tips

(These tips are courtesy of Linda and Rob Bjork.) You will need two baskets for the betting: one basket is the $1 basket, the other is the $5 basket.

The One Dollar Basket

Place the names of all the horses on slips of paper and put them in the basket. Have enough slips of paper so that each guest gets one slip. (Example if you have 32 guests and there are 16 horses running in the race, write out 32 slips using each horse's name twice.) Each guest draws a name and deposits a dollar. After the race, the guest, or guests, with the winning horse's name get to divide the pot.

The Five Dollar Basket

The host or hostess asks guests to deposit $5 in the basket. The host or hostess then writes down the guest's name and the name of the horse that guest believes will win the race. At the end of the race the guest, or guests, that picked the winning horse get to divide the pot.

The Party Plan

Invite a whole host of friends for a fun field trip to a nearby family compound or public park. Travel together by bus or van and offer appetizers and beverages along the way. Be sure to sing some favorite camp songs while en route. An afternoon of activity is planned, including an array of athletic events and an old-fashioned picnic. Arrange to play volleyball, badminton, bocce, croquet, horseshoes and have relay races. Swim to cool off afterwards. Splurge by supping on fabulous fare and then make s'mores around a huge bonfire or grill before heading back homewards.

Menu
Sallye Irvine - Bay Tables Cookbook

Bay Cooler Slush*

Savory Blue Cheesecake with French Bread Rounds*

Roast Beef Salad with Horseradish Vinaigrette*

Fresh Fruit

S'Mores

Recipe in the back of the book.

Pirogue holds dahlias, marigolds, fruit and bok choy.

A painted tin container is perfect for holding the wine along with an arrangement of bright, bold flowers.

zzy setting prime for picnicking.

Flair for the Affair

- Decorate the bus or van with streamers and giant paper flowers.
- Provide disposable cameras for everyone.
- Set up a scavenger hunt.
- Award silly prizes.

Décor and More

- Painted umbrellas
- Canvas placemats
- Colorful bandana napkins

Invitation Ideas

- A brightly colored mailing tube containing party details and a map.
- The party particulars printed on a bright bandana or card tied to a bandana.
- A miniature bok choy tied with ribbon and a card.

A stack of bright bandanas, plastic plates and polka-dotted tumblers make playful, practical picnic essentials.

Miniature bok choy serves as a unique invitation or place card.

Flower box favors.

How To

Painted Umbrella

Buy a white canvas umbrella. Thin gesso paint with water (2/3 gesso, 1/3 water). Put down a drop cloth and place the open umbrella low to the ground or in umbrella stand so it is easy to paint. Paint the entire umbrella with gesso and let dry. Start at the top of the umbrella and paint the pink, then blue, then two panels each of pink, orange and yellow. Let dry. Then add polka dots and basket designs. Let dry. After the paint is dry, spray with satin polyurethane to seal.

Hand-Painted Canvas Placemats

Purchase gesso-backed canvas, then outline the shape you want for your placemat and cut it out. Paint the placemat with a base color then, when dry, paint on the design. When paint dries spray with satin polyurethane to seal.

Painted canvas placemat.

Flower polka dot painted umbrella.

29

Summer

Summer is the season of sunshine — *filled with hot, happy days and warm, sultry nights. It is prime time for picnics and pool parties — for recreation, reunions and frolicking with friends and family. It is the time for enjoying the great outdoors and savoring such simple pleasures as swinging in a hammock, sipping on tropical drinks and splashing in the surf. Summer is also for indulging in old-fashioned treats, including fresh-squeezed lemonade, homemade ice cream and cold, sweet watermelon. Summer is enchanting — it brings out the child in everyone. Whether you are on vacation or staying close to home, summer is cheery, casual and just plain fun!*

The Party Plan

Invite your extended family for a fun, old-fashioned fish fry. This reunion is for reminiscing, along with eating and enjoying each other's company. Encourage everyone with musical talent to bring along instruments and hold an intergenerational jam session. Supply tamborines, maracas and other music makers for those that don't have their own instruments. Tell family stories and share cherished memories. Dust off that old-timey hand-cranked ice-cream maker and let the children take turns at the crank. After the feasting and festivities indulge in the freshly-churned ice cream served with a selection of beloved family desserts. Be sure to take plenty of pictures.

Menu
Kim Bremermann - Phydeaux's

Fresh Lemonade
Iced Tea
Charbroiled Mussels*
Artichokes Stuffed with Crawfish*
Fried Fish & Onion Rings
Old-Fashioned Coleslaw
Black Bottom Pie*
A Selection of Homemade Desserts and Ice Cream
Liver Pops for the Pups*

* Recipe in the back of the book.

Marigolds, impatiens, coleus and lisianthus clustered together look cool and pretty in a terra cotta saucer. It makes a great centerpiece.

elebration candelabra by Bev Church with Julia Yerkov s a fabulous, flamboyant ice cream cone holder. Flowers ucked into the cones of the pie server to add color.

Individual packets of hand wipes attached to newspaper clipping make a creative playful invite. (This invite was designed by The Stationer of New Orleans.)

|33

Instead of the classic newspaper covering, the table is draped with an antique rug. The table gets added pizzazz from a folk art fish sculpture and fish platters.

Flair for the Affair

- Hire a professional photographer to take photos of the entire clan as well as individual family shots.
- Have a recipe swap of "secret" family favorites. (Use these recipes to create a family recipe book to send out during the holidays.)
- Set up a table for displaying and viewing old scrapbooks and photo albums.

Miles Mumford with family dogs Sophia and Orcus at a reunion.

Décor and More

- Use antique birdhouses and family quilts as decoration.
- Bring out any fish-themed party paraphernalia to incorporate into the décor.
- Use terra cotta saucer centerpieces.

Invitation Ideas

- Hand wipes taped to the fish and game report.
- Copy an old family photo to use as the invite.
- Deliver an ice-cream cone filled with flowers and a note detailing the event.

A table set with an antique quilt and a delightful hodgepodge of folk art and family knickknacks looks cozy and inviting.

How To

Invitation

Glue a section of the newspaper onto a square piece of cardstock. Tape a package of hand wipes to the center and add a banner listing the time and date. The rest of the party particulars are on the back of the card.

Flowers in Saucer

Use a 10-inch terra cotta saucer and add several small "plugs" of plants. (Plugs of plants generally come in a 6-pack that can easily be pulled apart.) Pack the plants closely together. (We used marigolds, impatiens, coleus and lisianthus.)

Pool Party

36

The Party Plan

Summer is a great time for relaxing around the pool with friends — however, just because the setting is casual and the mood relaxed, it doesn't mean your party can't have plenty of pizzazz. Bring out the blender, festive barware and a selection of ingredients to allow guests to create their own smoothies or icy libations. Play summer favorites for mood music including Jimmy Buffet and Bob Marley. For added amusement, offer pool toys including noodles, rafts, balls and perhaps pool volleyball. (This party works especially well for the college-age set home on summer vacation as it provides an excellent opportunity for visiting and catching up with old friends and new — but it is truly tons of fun for any age group.)

ld pair of glass-paned doors painted
ua hues serves as a terrific tabletop
ith fun fish plates.

Menu
Upperline

Frozen Margaritas
Fruit Smoothies
Tomato and Onion Salad with Basil Dressing*
Grilled Fish with Upperline Salad Nicoise*
Tapenade*
Cornmeal Poundcake with Summer Berries*

Recipe in the back of the book.

Flower center piece.

Fish plates are placed on top of blue chargers. Under the blue chargers, we have used 14" diameter glass round chargers. This 1/4 inch thick glass was cut at a speciality glass shop. This will keep the blue chargers steady. We cut 8 glass rounds for our table.

Flair for the Affair

- Rent a margarita machine.
- Rent a jukebox.
- Whisk everyone away for a boat ride on the lake.

Décor and More

- Painted table
- Painted rug
- Chairback bouquets
- Watermelon service plates

Invitation Ideas

- Beach ball or inner tube invitation.
- Tie the invitation to a fish balloon.
- Fish bowl invitation with flowers.

Huge peppermint-striped poufs, each accented with a ladybug and sunflower, make festive chairback decorations.

How To

Painted Table
Use a large window or door, preferably a set of hinged doors. Paint the doors with white latex paint. Let dry. Then paint on a light coat of aquamarine paint thinned with water to create a streaked effect. Paint the panes of glass with paint purchased at the craft store specifically for use on glass or tile.

See doors on page 37.

We used frabic underneath the panes on page 36.

Painted Rug
To achieve a "bleached effect," roll two light coats of low-cost white latex paint onto an inexpensive or old sisal rug. When the paint is dry embellish with designs painted on with colorful acrylic paints. (We painted flowers and polka dots.)

Chairback Bouquets
Buy 3 yards of inexpensive, lightweight fabric per chair. Lay fabric down on the floor wrong side up. Fold in half then come down 17" from the top and gather towards the center. (See photograph.) Tie with a colorful ribbon. Stuff fabric with crumpled tissue paper or newsprint to create poufs. Hot glue flowers and faux bugs onto fabric. Hammer a nail into the back of a folding chair and hook on the chairback accent.

Painted rug.

Watermelon Service Plates
Slice a large watermelon into round slices, about 1½ to 2 inches in thickness. Place each round on a plate (use plates that are as close to the size of the melon as possible). Poke fresh flowers with sturdy stems in to the watermelon flesh close to the edge. (We used roses, lime green pompom chrysanthemums, geraniums and monticasino asters.) Serve food in ramekins or on plates atop the watermelon. Afterwards, the guests may eat the watermelon.

Watermelon service plate.

39

Fourth of July

THE PARTY PLAN

Invite 10 to 12 friends for a spirited Independence Day celebration. Energize the arrival by greeting guests at the gate with icy beverages, miniature flags and patriotic music. After some socializing and light snacking, serve a casual lunch starring an enormous, 6 foot, flag-studded po-boy or sub sandwich. The mid-day meal is followed by an afternoon of sporting events — doubles tennis matches and swimming. Then everyone heads out together to watch the parade. Finish your fabulous Fourth of July by enjoying an evening of cocktails and fireworks under the stars.

Menu
Mr. B's Bistro

Icy Bottles of Beer & Root Beer

Spinach, Strawberry & Ricotta Salata Salad*

Honey Ginger Barbequed Pork Chops*

Maque Choux*

Petite Blueberry Cheesecakes

Lemon Pie*

Recipe in the back of the book.

A Fourth of July napkin holder.

delphinium and iris with touches of white phlox in a -blown glass vase capped with a flag. Hand-painted rmelon slices are placed on the table for added decoration.

A patriotic party on the porch.

Faux flowers in appropriate hues rim a straw plate holder.

Flair for the Affair
- Serve a spiked watermelon.
- Have relay races with a greased watermelon.
- Rent a party pontoon boat for watching fireworks on the water.

Décor and More
- Fourth of July wreath
- Wooden watermelons
- Watermelon napkin rings

Invitation Ideas
- Tie a bunch of sparklers together with a card and red, white and blue ribbon.
- A red, white and blue card attached to a miniature flag.
- Deliver a whole watermelon wrapped with a big bow and the invitation attached.

An unexpected holiday wreath welcomes guests.

Individual cheesecakes dressed up with flag toothpicks.

How To

Wooden Watermelons

Buy 3/4-inch plywood that is good on both sides. Draw watermelons in several sizes on the wood and carefully cut out with a jigsaw. Sand the watermelon slices on both sides and along the edges. Paint the slices all over with gesso or white paint. Paint the watermelons with acrylic paint (red with a band of white or light green for the rind with green on the outer edge). When dry, paint seeds on the watermelon with black acrylic. When all the paint is dry, spray with polyurethane to seal.

Watermelon Napkin Rings

Make a pattern of a slice of watermelon and cut slices out of 3/4-inch plywood. Cut a hole in the center of each slice. Sand all over and follow the directions for wooden watermelons above.

Fourth of July Wreath

Soak a 10-inch oasis ring in water. Cut greenery into 2- to 3-inch long pieces (we used Japanese yew). Cover the ring with greenery by poking the ends into the oasis, then add clusters of red and white flowers (we used roses) in groups of three. Finish off with a grand red, white and blue bow. Secure to gate, fence or railing with wire. (Is also quite nice for hanging on a door or window.)

Caribbean Party

THE PARTY PLAN

Add some sizzle to the season by creating an incredible, island-inspired evening. During the height and heat of the summer, invite 20 to 30 guests to join you for dinner and dancing. Everyone arrives in tropical attire from tacky tourist to sexy sarongs. Line the entrance and the party perimeter with blazing torches to set a splendidly sultry mood. Invigorating steel band music fills the night air. Serve a buffet-style supper featuring tasty tropical fare and offer iced beers imported from the islands. After the dining is over, liven up the party by passing out maracas and encouraging everyone to dance and do the limbo.

buffet table offers a taste of the tropics metal palm trees, flowers and fruits.

Menu
Southern Hospitality Catering

Tropical Rum Punch
Iced Imported Beer
Jerk Chicken with Fried Plantains*
Caribbean Shrimp with Pineapple Rice*
Cuban Beef with Potatoes*
Key Lime Tarts
Chocolate Fountain with Fruit, Marshmallows and Coconut Cookies

* Recipe in the back of the book.

A metal mermaid sculpture makes another great centerpiece.

Icy bottles of beer and alternate beverages are served from a sarong-wrapped tub. And for a delightful classic touch of kitsch, tropical drinks are topped with colorful paper umbrellas.

Flair for the Affair
- Hire a steel band.
- Teach some hula movements.
- Be sure to have a limbo stick.

Décor and More
- Watermelon centerpiece
- Grass skirts for the tables
- Sarong-wrapped tubs for drinks
- Torches and luminaries

Invitation Ideas
- Twin bottles of Red Stripe beer in a basket filled with straw grass and a tropical card.
- Maracas tied with invite.
- A tape of island music along with invite.

Pretty tulips, tucked into a fish bowl, can easily serve as an invitation or a centerpiece.

Maracas for merry music-making.

How To

Grass Skirts for Cocktail Tables

For 30-inch cocktail tables, cut 45-inch circles out of burlap. Put the burlap on the tabletop and pin two grass skirts around the perimeter. Pin the skirts from the underside of the table so that the pins do not stick out or show.

Watermelon Centerpiece

Purchase a large, good-looking watermelon. Slice a small portion off of one end so that the watermelon is able to stand up straight and tall. Place the watermelon on a plate so that it will not drip on your table. Cut the top off the watermelon and scoop out the heart of the watermelon (save it to snack on later). Fill a clean mayonnaise jar with water and place into the scooped out melon shell. Add tropical flowers of varying heights.

The tropical setting with grass skirt cocktail tables. Thanks to Kevin Gillentine and Vincent Bergeal for creating the grass shack and painting of the beach.

Watermelon centerpiece.

Biking Bash

The Party Plan

Savor those last delicious days of late summer, when the weather cools ever so slightly, by planning a biking trek with 6 to 10 biking buddies. Start the festivities by decorating the basket of the lead bike. Bring along bottles of water and some light snacks for the road. At the halfway point, stop for a spot of socializing and refueling before the return journey. End the afternoon at a favorite watering hole or tavern where you can all relax and refresh. Play pool, darts and dance to the jukebox, then enjoy drinks and casual dinner.

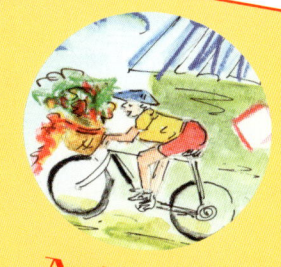

Menu
Rivershack

Chilled Sports Drinks
Ice Water
Cold Beer
Blackened Shrimp Remoulade
Fried Green Tomato Salad Napoleon with Lump Crabmeat*
Herb Vinaigrette Dressing*
Fried Louisiana Quail with Crawfish and Corn Maque Choux*
Souther Comfort Bread Pudding with Cassis Cream*

*Recipe in the back of the book.

Faux flower covered candleholder.

server doubles as a flower holder for red hybiscus blooms.
flowers perk up a candleholder and shade.

The invite tied with a toy bike.

Flair for the Affair

- Pick a night when a band is playing at the chosen end location.
- Have a truck or van at the end point to take everyone home. (Or start and end at the tavern.)
- Have non-biking friends and spouses meet you for the after party to join in the fun.
- Have everyone decorate their bikes.

Décor and More

- Decorated bike basket
- Flower-covered candleholders

Invitation Ideas

- Sports bottle with invitation attached.
- A toy bicycle with invitation attached.
- Trail mix and invitation tied with a ribbon.

Casual napkins in wooden pear napkin rings add a happy touch. A comical bit of sound advice on a hand-painted sign by Dr. Bob. (Placemats by Ray Cole).

How To

Decorated Bike Basket
Use 4 yards of 3-inch ribbon to tie around bike basket and into a great big bow. Add a couple of papier mâché flowers (ours are designed by Ida Rak).

Flower-Covered Candleholders
Buy small candleholders with metal shades. Hot glue a variety of faux greens and flowers to base, stem and shade of the candleholder.

A decorated basket filled with flowers and bottles of water marks the lead bicycle. The smiling band of bikers ready for their ride.

A flower-filled, painted wheelbarrow by Dr. Bob at the Rivershack in New Orleans.

An Al Fresco Event

THE PARTY PLAN

Gather together your garden club or 16 to 20 gardening buddies for a glorious afternoon in the great outdoors. Set up a variety of al fresco vignettes on the porch, the patio and throughout the yard. Serve a light lunch followed by an extravagant flaming dessert. Encourage each of the guests to pick the place that best suits their personality from among the offered open-air settings. For extra fun, have everyone change to a different venue for the dessert course. (This party works best when two or more friends combine their talents, as the set up involves substantial, yet tremendously enjoyable, preparation and planning.)

Menu
Bella Luna, Brennan's and Commander's Palace

White Sangria
Iced Red Zinger Tea
Brennan's Vichyssoise Vieux Carré*
Bella Luna's Creole Crab and Crawfish Cakes with Ancho Aioli*
Commander's Palace Shrimp & Tasso with Five Pepper Jelly*
Brennan's Lemon Curd Tartelette*

* Recipe in the back of the book.

Flowers in a pretty lettuce vase.

A fabulous floral scene featuring oversized globes of faux Gerbera daisies hanging from the chairs and trees, a flower-festooned tablecloth and a brilliant green watering can brimming with blooms. (Leaf placemats are by Ray Cole.)

A fern-covered box makes a marvelous invitation.

Banana tree flower holders, designed by Bev Church with Julia Yerkov, are a delightful centerpiece atop a colorful oil cloth. Flowery oil cloth totes filled with bright tissue contain favors for everyone.

Iced tea for two on a hand-hokked rug. Aprons are used as napkins.

Flair for the Affair

- Request that everyone wear hats (preferably adorned with flowers).
- Ask that each guest bring cuttings from their favorite plants for sharing (including botanical names and growing instructions).
- Encourage everyone to bring favorite recipes featuring freshly picked goodies from the garden.

Invitation Idea

- Flower garden gloves in a fern-covered box
- A diminutive faux flower ball with invite attached for hanging on a doorknob.
- A small box of rye grass with a flower in a pick with a leaf card attached outlining party particulars.

Décor and More

- Tablecloth with floral edging
- Leaf tablecloth
- Hanging flower balls

How To

Tablecloth with Floral Edging

Choose an inexpensive cloth that fits the table you are using. Start with about 20 to 30 assorted silk flowers. Disassemble the leaves and flowers of some of the flowers. Hot glue an assortment of green leaves around the perimeter of the cloth. Then glue a variety of petals all around the edge, combining different colors and textures as you go along. Every now and then glue a whole flower to the mix. (See pages 52 and 107.)

An elegant vignette on the patio with a leaf-laden tablecloth and a lofty, graceful arrangement of holly fern, pink asters, campanula and yellow roses. (Leaf centerpiece designed by Bev Church and Julia Yerkov.)

Leaf Tablecloth

Buy an inexpensive green tablecloth or piece of green fabric to fit your table. Hot glue an assortment of different greenery onto the cloth, starting with the perimeter and working your way to the center, overlapping the leaves a little bit as you go, until the cloth is completely covered.

Hanging Flower Balls (small and large)

You may use styrofoam balls in any size you like. Stick faux flowers into the styrofoam until it is covered completely. Then insert a screw eye into the tops of the styrofoam ball. Tie a ribbon through the eye and hang.

Fern-Covered Box

Buy several 4"x 4"x 4" white cake boxes at a party supply store. Assemble the boxes, then spray them with basil-colored paint. (We used Design Master.) Hot glue faux fern fronds and purple pansies to the boxes.

Garden Gloves

Hot glue bright silk blossoms to the top, outside edge of each glove.

Garden-variety gloves gone glamorous with the addition of snappy faux flowers.

Autumn

Autumn

Autumn is gloriously golden.
The brisk chill in the air is invigorating. It is sweater weather. It is the time for tailgating, for football games and for collegiate camaraderie. Fall is also when the cultural season starts to soar bringing with it music, arts and infinite opportunities for celebrating with friends — for sipping cider, for picking the perfect pumpkin and for gathering around the grill. It is a season of harvest, and of hunting. A time for partaking in nature's rich bounty — lush, ripe produce and majestic, wild game.

57

Farmer's Market Dinner

The Party Plan

A satisfying, productive trip to the farmer's market provides the fodder for this delectable dinner with close friends. Meet up with a friend, or another couple, for the morning foray to the market. Revel in the abundant array of produce, selecting the freshest, most enticing foods and flowers in anticipation of the evening to come. Let the available items inspire the menu and the décor for the gathering. The afternoon is spent together cooking an appetizing meal and creating attractive surroundings. Invite 4 to 6 additional guests to join you in enjoying the final results and fruits of your labor.

The buffet table set up in the courtyard overflows with an opulent array of fresh flowers and produce.

The regal ivy-covered candelabra is a permanent resident in the courtyard. It is always primed for a party, just add candles and light.

Menu

Antoine's

Chilled Local or Regional White & Red Wines

Bouillabaisse*

Chateaubriand with Marchand de Vins Sauce Champignons*

Sauté of Fresh Vegetables

Hot Bread

Strawberries with Kirsch*

* Recipe in the back of the book.

...ers at the farmer's market.

Cabbages, golden bell peppers, carrots and a whole host of other colorful produce are interspersed with flowers and candles in the lavish arrangement.

Flair for the Affair

- Hire a street performer from the market to play music or entertain for 30 minutes during cocktails.
- Give everyone a small basket and allow them to pluck some produce from the arrangements to take home.
- Purchase preserves from the market, tie with a ribbon and present as party favors.

Décor and More

- Pepper and or gourd vases
- Ivy-covered candelabra
- Lavish table display

Invitation Ideas

- A little basket of fall produce with invitation tucked inside.
- A gourd or small pumpkin with invitation tied to the stem.
- A small bundle of fresh flowers with invitation attached.

An earthenware urn bursting with delphinium, hot pink and red Gerbera daisies, and lady's mantle with ivy added.

How To

Pepper or Gourd Vases

Make sure the gourd or pepper can stand up – if not, slice a small bit off the bottom to stabilize. (If you slice off the bottom, be sure to place a plate underneath.) Then cut the top off of a gourd or pepper. Clean out the center and add a small, clean jar filled with water or a small, soaked square of oasis. Add desired flowers.

Lavish Table Display

Cover the table with fresh greenery, clipped from the garden. (We used fatsia, kale and aspidistra). Place large serving pieces on the table. Add candles and/or candelabra. Add the arrangement of flowers in the gourd. Then, working around the pieces, allowing a little bit of room, mound the peppers, gourds, pumpkins and lemons on and around the greenery.

A glossy yellow pepper filled with flowers.

Blowout Barn Party

THE PARTY PLAN

Autumn is the ideal occasion to host a glamorous, gussied-up barn party. Stock the barn with an abundance of seasonal accents, including piles of pumpkins, towering corn stalk teepees and cheery, checkered cloths to make the voluminous surroundings cozy and inviting. Add in some dramatic, sky-high flower arrangements, for a stylish twist. Call together a crowd of 30 or 40 guests to share in this swanky shindig. Start the evening off by offering cocktails and appetizers in the garden. Then swing open the barn doors for hours of dining and dancing. Hire an accordion player or Cajun combo to serenade guests. End the evening by transporting everyone via horse-drawn wagon to a roaring bonfire. (The inspiration and photographs for this most memorable evening came from a party given by Bev's dear friends, Elizabeth and Clarke Swanson, at their vineyard in California.)

Menu
Swanson Vineyards

Swanson Pinot Grigio
Swanson Merlot
Swanson Angelica
Smoked Salmon with Lemon Zest and Dill on Crostini with Crème Fraiche
Creole Tomato Soup with Green Onion and Sour Cream*
Stuffed Pork Tenderloin with Sweet potatoes*
Fig Tart with Almond Mascarpone*

Recipe in the back of the book.

Artichoke surrounded by nerine lilies and zebra zinnias.

lean tables are piled with pumpkins and gourds, and lined fabulous, fall flower arrangements, standing tall.

A wagon drawn by two workhorses takes guests to the awaiting bonfire.

A towering tee-pee of hay is surrounded by pumpkins and gourds.

Flair for the Affair
- Hire someone to give dance instructions and/or to call a square dance.
- Have a jukebox available for playing favorite tunes during band breaks.
- Arrange a hayride with a horse-drawn wagon to transport guests to the bonfire.

Décor and more
- Bandana napkins
- Sprinkle candy corn all over the table.
- Decorate with hay and dried corn stalks.
- Use large gourds and pumpkins lined up as centerpieces.

Invitation Ideas
- Little burlap bags filled with candy corn with invite attached.
- Small pumpkins or gourds with the invitation inscribed in gold ink.
- An elegant card tied to a tiny hay bale.

Bright bandanas are nifty, theme-appropriate napkins.

How To

Bandana Napkins

Buy bandanas in bulk at low cost. Fold each bandana into a triangle. Gather together so that it poufs at the top. Tie with a ribbon — into a bow or pretty knot (see photograph).

Corn stalks, cherry tomato vines and dahlias make a lovely, lofty seasonal display.

Girl's Night Out

THE PARTY PLAN

Autumn marks the annual advent of the cultural season — when the symphony, ballet, opera and countless other arts events start up again after a long, sweltering summer hiatus. It is a time of great anticipation and excitement. Unfortunately, all-too-often the gentlemen are absent during this time of the year attending football games or hunting. So, this evening is designed as a girl's night out but could easily be a celebration for couples, as well. (Our party was created as an elegant buffet supper before the opera, *Madame Butterfly* by Puccini at Becky Currence's home.) Invite friends to arrive two hours prior to the performance. Imbibe wonderful wine, then serve the scrumptious buffet. Offer coffee, lightly-laced with liqueur, as a pleasing pick-me-up before heading out for the much-awaited entertainment.

Menu
Martin Wine Cellar
Chilled Chablis
Artichoke Risotto Cakes*
Marinated Grilled Vegetables*
Boudin Stuffed Cornish Hens with Tabasco Pepper Jelly Glaze*
Coffee with Amaretto and Whipped Cream
* Recipe in the back of the book.

Flowers and lanterns hanging in the trees.

The serving table looks exquisite all aglow with glittering candles and shining sterling silver.

Elaborate antique salt and pepper shakers and Chaffe McIlhenny goblets of sapphire glass add ornate touches amid the shimmering votive candles and a trio of crystal vases featuring completely open Miranda roses and tulips.

Flair for the Affair

- Arrange for a driver, or a limousine, to chauffeur everyone to and from the event.
- Present each guest with a beautiful fan.
- Play music from the performance you are preparing to attend.

Décor and More

- Bring out all your finest — silver, china and crystal.
- Light candles everywhere.
- Hang paper lanterns and flower-filled vases from the trees.
- Set up an elegant bar.
- Ivy sprays on the chairbacks.

Invitation Ideas

- An invitation designed as a program.
- A CD of music from the performance you are attending with invite attached.
- A fan with the invite attached to the handle or written on the fan in gold ink.

Plump Cornish game hens and petite filets with marinated grilled vegetables.

A wine cart, swathed in fabric intertwined with ivy, serves as an elegant bar.

How To

Flower Vases

Cut sheer ribbon in 4', 6' and 8-foot lengths. Then drape the ribbons over desired tree branches at varying heights. Then, tie the ribbons through the hook on the vase holders (designed by Bev Church with Julia Yerkov) and insert the vases filled with flowers.

Wrapping the Wine Cart

Start with a piece of fabric 10 to 12 feet in length. Tuck the selvage edges under so they can't be seen and lay the fabric down flat on top of the cart or table to be used. Create a pouf of fabric at one end and secure it with a rubberband. Let the remaining fabric cascade down to the ground. Tuck long lengths of ivy into the cloth and arrange so that ivy cascades down as well.

Chairback Ivy Sprays

Cut ivy in lengths a little bit longer than the length of the chairtop. Wind the greenery in and out. Secure in place by using a little bit of green floral wire, if necessary.

Luminous paper lanterns and floating flowers create a memorable, magical dining area.

Posh Polo Party

THE PARTY PLAN

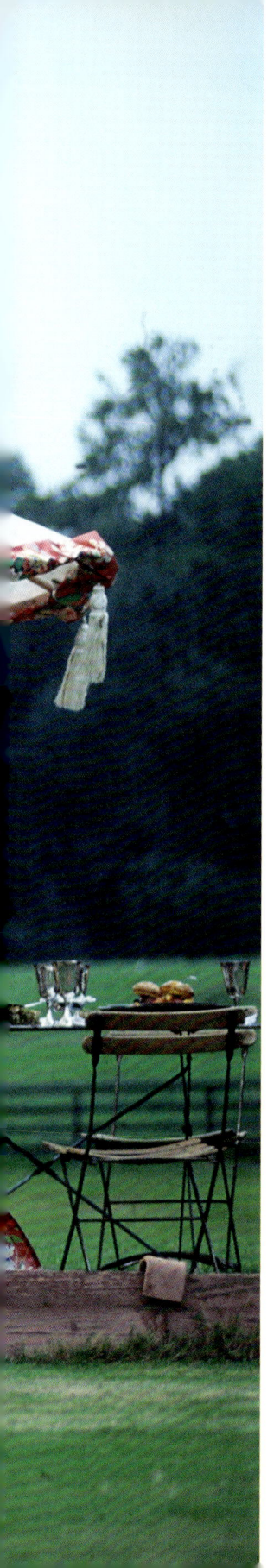

Tailgating is the classic moveable feast. It is a festive fall ritual that makes the perfect party for both pre- and post- sporting events — taken perhaps to its pinnacle at a posh polo match. To make the tailgating ultra toney, tote along a market umbrella, a folding table or two, and several chairs. Upon arrival, set up your entertaining area and drape the tabletops and chairs with chic fabric. It is also important to upgrade from the usual disposables to the utmost refined accoutrements including silver cutlery, goblets, fine china and damask napkins — the whole nine yards, and then some. Sip champagne and nibble on hors d'oeuvres while spectating and socializing. Afterwards dine luxuriously on a banquet that has been previously prepared — by you, a quality caterer, or onsite by a chef. (Thanks to Jennifer Rice and the Junior League of Covington.)

Lovely ladies in their chic chapeaux sip champagne while watching the polo match.

Menu
Artesia

Champagne
Pimm's Cup
Artesia Salad with Lobster
Spiced Pecans*
Layered Brie with Assorted Breads & Crackers*
Maple Sage Sausage*
Blueberry and Cream Cheese Bread Pudding*

* Recipe in the back of the book.

Baguettes, champagne and a quintet of slim flower arrangements make a tasteful, terrific table.

Flair for the Affair

- Roll out the Oriental carpets for deluxe ground cover.
- Hire a chef to prepare your meal match-side.
- Bring along the makings for a signature drink, such as Pimm's Cup or dessert martinis.

Décor and more

- Tasseled umbrella
- Tablecloth and chair covers

Invitation Ideas

- Write the details on the back of your engraved calling card and slip the card under the golden elastic on a tiny four-piece box of fine chocolates.
- Tie an elegant printed invitation to a horseshoe spray-painted either silver or gold.
- A split of champagne with invite attached.

Famed polo player, Charles Schroeder, prepares to mix up a Pimm's Cup. Jennifer Rice's two Cavalier King Charles Spaniels — Molly being held and Emily on the carpet watching the polo match.

An autumnal arrangement includes red coffee beans, blue lace flowers, yellow spray roses and basil-colored sedum.

How To

Tassled Umbrella

Measure the circumference of a huge market umbrella. Add an extra 2 feet to the measurement to determine how much fabric you need. Fold the fabric in half so that you can only see the "good side." Then using hat pins, tack the fabric in place on the perimeter of the umbrella, twisting slightly as you go. Pin tassels on for accents.

A pot of golden mums in a champagne bucket makes a simple, classic arrangement on the table set for four.

Wild Game Dinner

The Party Plan

During the height of hunting season plan a splendid seated supper for sharing the spoils of the hunt. This time it is the men who don the aprons and prepare the feast. The ladies are in charge of decorating and dessert. Request that each of the gentlemen bring along their favorite recipe — be it gumbo or appetizers, prepared in advance, or venison or gamebirds ready for the grill. Serve deep, dark, delicious red wines to complement the robust flavor of fresh wild game. The evening is spent savoring each other's company and a hearty autumnal repast.

Menu
Bella Luna

Robust Red Wines

Fall Greens in Cranberry Vinaigrette with Roasted Pecans and Blue Cheese*

Grilled Butternut Squash Soup*

Venison Tenderloin in Beer Glaze*

Stuffed Crêpes with Apples and Caramel Sauce*

Recipe in the back of the book.

...lous Gien pheasant china on a ...er charger makes an elegant place setting.

A wild game dinner gone glamorous.

A pavéd rose centerpiece featuring opulent, completely open Osciana and First Gold roses in an ivy-covered container.

Flair for the Affair
- Announce each course by using a duck call.
- Present guests with favor boxes containing a jar of glaze good for using on game.
- Provide personalized aprons for the men to wear and then take home.

Décor and More
- Decorate with copper and metal serving pieces along with anything sporting: a duck, pheasant, or similar motif.
- Wild grass chairback bouquets
- Ribbon-wrapped favor boxes
- Pavéd rose centerpiece

Invitation Ideas
- A paper toque (chef's hat) with the invitation written on the band.
- Invitation tied to a duck call.
- Aspidistra and grasses tied together with a bow, invite is written on the leaves.

How To

Wild Grass Chairback Bouquets with Greenery

Gather together an assortment of wild grasses and greenery. (We used aspidistra, wheat, exotic grasses and bear grass, both fresh and dried.) Secure the bundle of grasses with green floral wire. Wrap the wire with thin gold cording to cover and tie the bouquets to the backs of chairs in two places.

Ribbon-Wrapped Favor Boxes

Purchase 4"x 4"x 4" cake boxes. Wrap each box with an 11-inch long piece of 11-inch wide wired ribbon and secure with a rubberband (see photograph). Place a wrapped box on each guest's chair or at their place setting.

Pavéd Rose Centerpiece

Soak a 27-inch piece of oasis in water. Start by covering the sides with ivy and rose leaves. Then cut the roses, leaving stems about 1½ to 2 inches in length, and add the blooms to the top until oasis is entirely covered. (Be sure to protect your table by placing plastic or foil under the tray the oasis comes in. A piece of mirror underneath, cut slightly larger than the arrangement, is especially pretty.)

Fresh and dried wild grasses gathered together, form a spectacular chairback bouquet.

A favor box wrapped in golden, gossamer ribbon.

Black & White Bash

THE PARTY PLAN

A black and white bash is a stunning, dramatic way to celebrate an engagement. It is also an excellent way to honor a debutante during her season or mark an important wedding anniversary. A black and white tent at the entrance, along with a tented dance floor, sets the stage for a very special night. Black and white cocktails and cuisine are the order for the evening including black and white sushi, zebra-striped pasta, and chocolate and vanilla petit fours. A table on the front porch with black or white martinis adds a chic touch to the swanky soirée. Have a band or piano player provide music for tripping the light — black and white — fantastic. Pass champagne for toasting at midnight. (This party was originally created to celebrate the engagement of Bev's son, John Mark and his bride, Dottie Gibbons.)

...with painted dance floor awaiting the guests. ...al thanks to Luis Colmenares in New Orleans.

Menu
Southern Hospitality Catering

Champagne

Black & White Martinis

Black & White Salad*

Black & White Zebra-Striped Bow Tie Pasta Alfredo with Gulf Shrimp*

Dark Chocolate Mousse with White Topping*

* Recipe in the back of the book.

An alternative invitation idea.

This clever invitation designed by Betty Hunley of New Orleans proclaiming that The Excitement will be "InTents"!

Flair for the Affair
- Hire a pianist to play requests and favorite dance tunes.
- Have several black and white boas on hand for anyone who wants to perform.
- Arrange to have a martini table or an ice sculpture designed to hold chilled black caviar and vodka.
- Serve spiked white hot chocolate or café brûlot from a samovar.
- Hire someone to draw caricatures of the guests.

Décor and More
- Party perimeter and walkways lit with luminaries or torchieres.
- Zebra squares for accents
- Tents everywhere
- Painted dance floor
- Oversized caricatures of the honoree or honorees.

Invitation Ideas
- A fabulous black and white printed invitation.
- A black and a white balloon tied with mylar ribbon to a black card written with silver pen.
- A martini glass with invitation attached.

The dramatic entrance, tented in black and white, features full-sized caricatures of the hono Caricatures of Dottie and John Mark created by Arthur Fischer.

How To

Zebra Squares

Wrap a 14-inch cardboard cake square with zebra fabric cut into a 17-inch square (this allows an inch and a half overlap). Fold under the corners and hot glue. Then hot glue the sides, being careful to stretch the fabric taut so there are no wrinkles.

Painted Dance Floor

Hire a professional to cover your pool. Get approval to paint plywood with your custom design. First, paint wood with white latex base coat. Let dry. Paint scrolls, vines and leaves, or as desired. Tip: Fasten paint brush to 3 ft. to 4 ft. pole with tape to make it easier to paint.

Snazzy zebra-striped squares, glittering votives and a myriad of white mums line the walkway.

The divine dance floor painted by Luis Colmenares of New Orleans showcases the engaged couple's initials amongst the fanciful black scrolls.

Winter

Winter

Winter starts with a myriad of sparkling celebrations. Everything is aglow and aglitter. It is a time of twinkling lights, joyous songs and excitement. It is a time for traditions and for basking in the presence of treasured friends and family. Then the new year makes its debut amid much toasting and champagne. The luxurious lull, after the bustling holiday whirl, is a splendid time to snuggle up with loved ones in front of a crackling fire. This is a cozy period of rejuvenation during the cold hush of deepest winter — before the revelry and mirth of Mardi Gras and the romance and sentiment of St. Valentine's Day.

Holiday Progressive Party

THE PARTY PLAN

This whirlwind progressive party is a grand way to entertain a gregarious, intergenerational group during the holiday season. Several families work together to stage this merry evening. The party starts in the late afternoon. At the first house, everyone engages in gingerbread house construction; hot cocoa is served, along with an array of add-ins including liqueurs, whipped cream, cinnamon, peppermint sticks and so forth. At the second stop, the children dine on pizza while the adults enjoy appetizers and each other's company. At the third destination, the adults are treated to a fancy seated dinner while the children, accompanied by teenagers, head out for some old-fashioned, neighborhood caroling. Everyone reunites after dinner for dessert, coffee and more singing.

Menu
Arnaud's

French 75 Cocktail*

Champagne

Mushrooms Veronique*

Arnaud's Oyster Soup*

Filet of Veal or Beef Chantal with Micro Greens and Champagne Vinaigrette*

Crêpes Suzette

Hot Cocoa & Coffee

Recipe in the back of the book.

A Santa ornament is a favor as well as a place card.

A gingerbread village enchants the children.

The pillar candle glows amid a ring of roses and red carnations.

stunning holiday table set for a seated dinner.

85

Flair for the Affair
- Give note cards tied with tulle as party favors for post-holiday thank you notes.
- Have sheet music of favorite songs available for the carolers.
- Pass out Santa hats or reindeer ears for the carolers to wear.
- Have funny prizes for the gingerbread houses as "Best use of nuts in a design" or "Best chimney," etc.

Décor and More
- Decorate the chandelier.
- Use lots of twinkling white lights.
- Pine tree chairbacks
- Apple place cards
- Yew topiaries with red Gerbera daisies
- Pillar candles with flower rings

Invitation Ideas
- Gingerbread house cookie attached to the invitation.
- A pine bough tied with a big holiday bow along with the invite.
- Roll up Christmas sheet music along with invite and tie with a holiday ribbon.

Pine trees tied with ribbons and ornamented with flowers make dramatic decorations.

How To

Pillar Candles with Flower Rings

Soak a 10- to 12-inch oasis ring in water for a few minutes. Add roses and carnations to the ring, alternating the flowers to achieve the desired effect. Place the ring on a dish and add candle and hurricane globe to the center. Water ring often to keep flowers fresh.

Pine Tree Chairback Bouquets

Cut pine tree branches about 5 feet to 6 feet tall and soak the cut edge in water overnight. After soaking, wrap the cut ends in clear plastic wrap (to keep the sap from oozing onto your floor or rug). Tie a branch to the back of each chair in at least two places using ribbon (we used red and hot pink). Wire together three to five flowers to create mini nosegays and wire these to the branches (we used roses and carnations). Use approximately five nosegays per tree.

Yew Topiaries with Red Gerbera Daisies

Soak cone-shaped oasis in water. (You may carve a cone shape out of a block of oasis if you choose.) Beginning at the top of the cone, add cuttings of yew (about 2 to 3 inches in length) until the oasis is completely covered and resembles a tree. Place the tree on a plate, saucer or into a decorative container. Add red flowers as accent. (We used red Gerbera daisies.)

Yew topiaries with red Gerbera daisies.

House Party

The Party Plan

Mid-winter is a glorious time to invite out-of-town friends for a warm, wonderful weekend house party to renew ties and spend some splendid quality time together. Arrange for your guests to arrive in the late morning on Saturday, serve them lunch at home by the fire, then venture out for an afternoon of activities. Go sightseeing, antiquing or visit a museum. Return home to refresh before a night on the town. Invite other friends to join you at your favorite bowling alley. (We love Rock'n' Bowl in New Orleans.) End the evening at home with popcorn and an old classic movie. The next morning, treat your overnight guests to breakfast with a French flair. Afterwards, relax, read the newspaper and play cards – enjoying a leisurely visit before an afternoon departure.

Menu
Gabrielle

Viognier or Sancerre Wines

Hot Buttered Rum

Oyster Stew*

Grillades & Roasted Pepper Grits*

Apple Upside-Down Bread Pudding with Vanilla Bean Sauce*

Recipe in the back of the book.

Small French soap favor in front of bird of paradise napkin fold.

...at home with flowers adorning ...vent pastries of all sizes.

A warm, welcoming table set French-style for breakfast. Thanks to Custom Linens in New Orleans

89

Flair for the Affair

- Have favors for your guests at each meal.
- Buy baseball caps for everyone and personalize with each name and the date of the party.
- Place a silver tray by each bedside complete with bottled water, flowers and treats.

Décor and More

- Flowers in a vol au vent
- Flowers in a candlestick
- Armbands for the bowling alley

Snazzy papier mâché alligators by Katie Rafferty dancing on the tabletop.

Invitation Ideas

- Send a box filled with local flavor (we sent beignet mix, hot sauce and jambalaya mix) along with invite and a tentative itinerary detailing plans and attire for the weekend.
- Send a map of the town with your house marked in bright pen along with invite, and other particulars.
- Send a tape of local music along with invite.

A fun fish centerpiece is surrounded by a sea of party favors at Rock'n' Bowl.

How To

FLOWERS IN A VOL AU VENT
Carefully cut the top off of a puff pastry (we used a vol au vent). Scoop out the bread, if necessary. Add a small glass or jar, filled with water-soaked oasis, and arrange desired flowers in it. (We used dahlias, hydrangeas, statice and chinaberry.)

FLOWERS IN A CANDLESTICK
Buy an o'daptor (oasis shaped to fit in a candlestick) from the florist or floral supply. Soak the o'daptor, then add flowers to cover.

ARMBANDS
Cut chosen ribbon in lengths about 15 inches long. Hot glue flowers on the armbands for the girls. (Give armbands of plain ribbon to the men.)

Big, bright blooms atop a whimsical ceramic candlestick.

Armbands help the bartenders and waitstaff distinguish the guests from the rest of the crowd.

An Evening of Amour

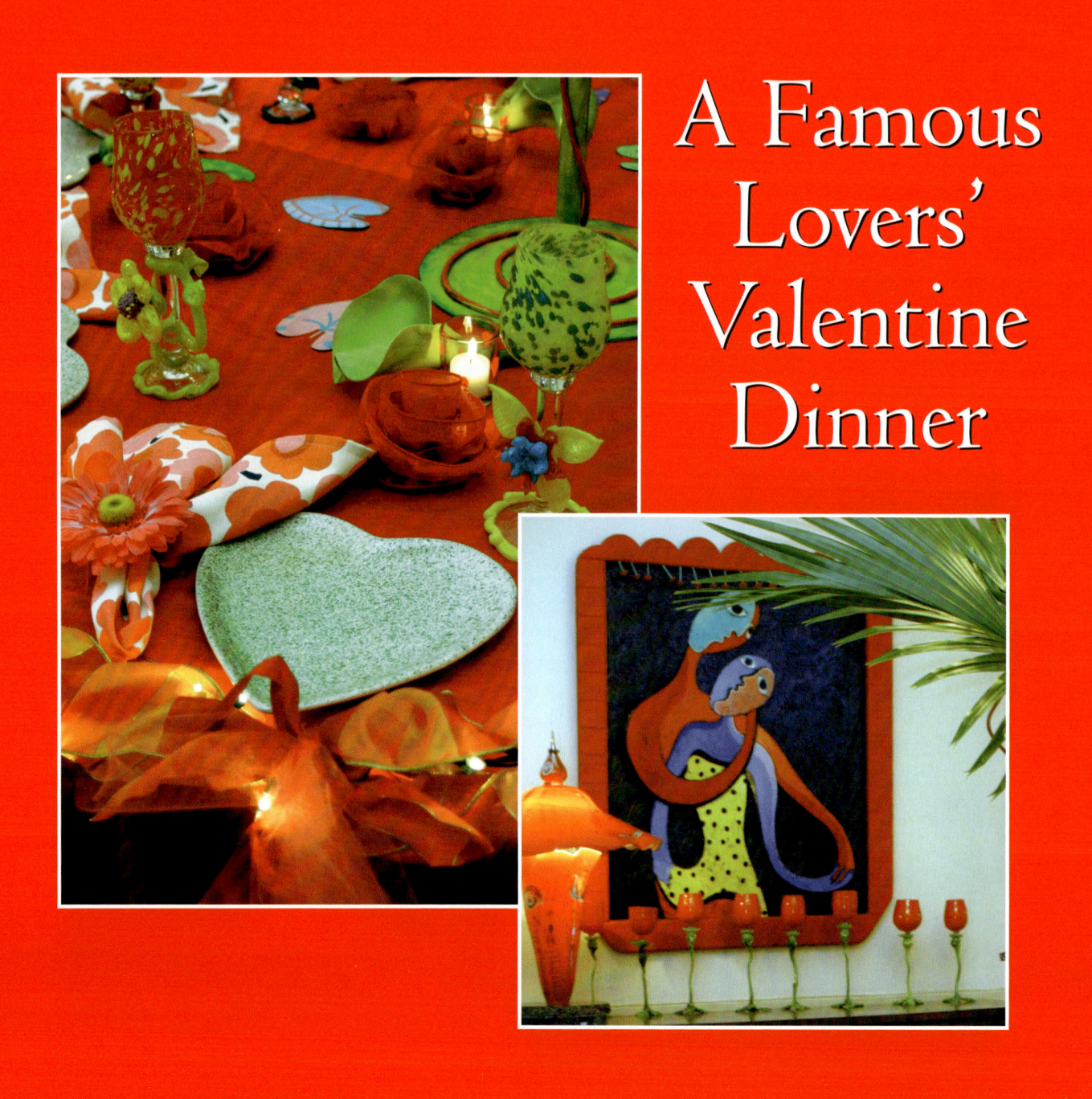

A Famous Lovers' Valentine Dinner

THE PARTY PLAN

Invite 2 or 3 couples to join you for a romantic repast on Valentine's evening. Request that everyone come costumed as famous lovers throughout the ages — Desi and Luci, Napoleon and Josephine, Cleopatra and Mark Antony, Romeo and Juliet, Richard Burton and Elizabeth Taylor, Rhett and Scarlett, and so forth. Ask that no one reveal their identities until the other guests have had a chance to guess. Take photographs of each couple upon their arrival. (The picture will be placed in frames for party favors.) Serve a memorable meal including such infamous aphrodisiacs as champagne, asparagus, oysters, and chocolate. Then dance the night away!

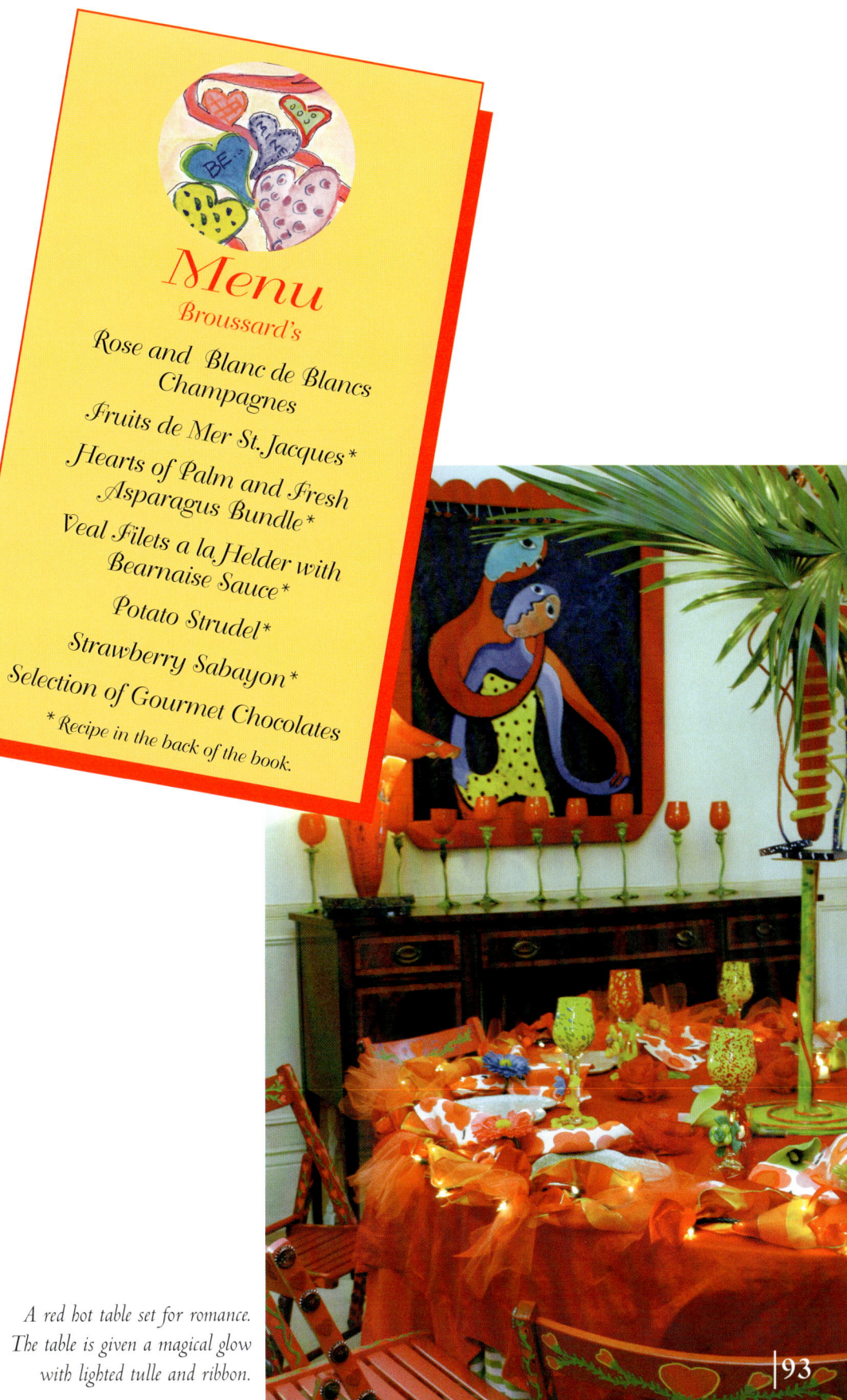

Menu
Broussard's

Rose and Blanc de Blancs Champagnes

Fruits de Mer St. Jacques*

Hearts of Palm and Fresh Asparagus Bundle*

Veal Filets a la Helder with Bearnaise Sauce*

Potato Strudel*

Strawberry Sabayon*

Selection of Gourmet Chocolates

Recipe in the back of the book.

...t shaped plates and handblown glasses
...eri Walker jazz up the table.
...ainting "Lovers" is by Luis Cogley.
... and wine glasses by artist Andrew Brott.

A red hot table set for romance. The table is given a magical glow with lighted tulle and ribbon.

Flair for the Affair
- Greet guests with flutes filled with rose champagne.
- Play mood music all night long including Etta James, Frank Sinatra, Dean Martin and more.
- Slow dance between courses.
- Engrave silver frames with the date for party favors.

Décor and More
- Ribbon roses
- Illuminated tulle for the table
- Flower napkin rings
- Painted tin hearts
- Tray with flowers and chocolates

Invitation Ideas
- Heart-shaped boxes of chocolate truffles with invite attached.
- A single long-stemmed red rose with the invite attached with red silk ribbon.
- An invitation featuring a famous, passionate couple sealed in an envelope filled with red hots.

How To

Ribbon Roses

Buy wired ribbon in two designs. (We used an opaque red and a sheer red.) One of the ribbons should be 1½ to 2 inches wide and the other should be 3 to 4 inches wide. Cut the ribbons into yard-long segments. Starting with one side of the ribbon, pull the fabric of the ribbon so it is gathered tightly together on one side. As you pull, knot the wire on the other end so that it won't pull completely out of the ribbon. Turn the gathered pieces and wrap them around your finger, forming the rose as you go. When the rose is the desired size, tie off the end, then sew the ribbon rose together in several places so that it will not unravel.

A heart-shaped plate holds a red ribbon rose.

Tray with Flowers and Chocolates

Choose a tray/platter that is 8" x 10". Cut a piece of heavy cardboard 6" x 8" and cover with plastic to protect tray. Then cut water soaked oasis in 1" high pieces and arrange them to cover the area perfectly. Oasis comes in blocks that are 9" x 4½" x 3". Cut the oasis lengthwise 1" x 9" x 3" and cut 2 pieces. Slice 1" off the bottom of each piece so you end up with 1" x 8" x 3". Put them together side by side and you end up with 1" x 8" x 6". Buy 2 bunches of sunflower pompom chrysanthemums — we used 42 of them to cover oasis completely. Cut the flowers so that they have 3/4" stems and polk them into the oasis. When ready to serve, place the chocolate pieces on top.

Tray with flowers and chocolates.

A Moveable Mardi Gras

The Party Plan

You needn't be in New Orleans, Mobile or Rio de Janeiro to take part in the incomparable mirth of Mardi Gras. Fat Tuesday can be celebrated anywhere – all you need is the spirit – and a suitcase packed with party essentials. Invite a dozen or so revelers to participate in a moveable Mardi Gras. As each guest enters, hand them a libation and place several strands of beads around their neck. Then pass around a hat or bowl with slips of paper – the duo that receive the slips marked king and queen get special attire for the event including scepters, crowns and capes. As everyone sits down to dine, ask them to don their masks. After dinner, everyone grabs their napkins to second-line with the king and queen leading the parade. Finish with king cake and dancing.

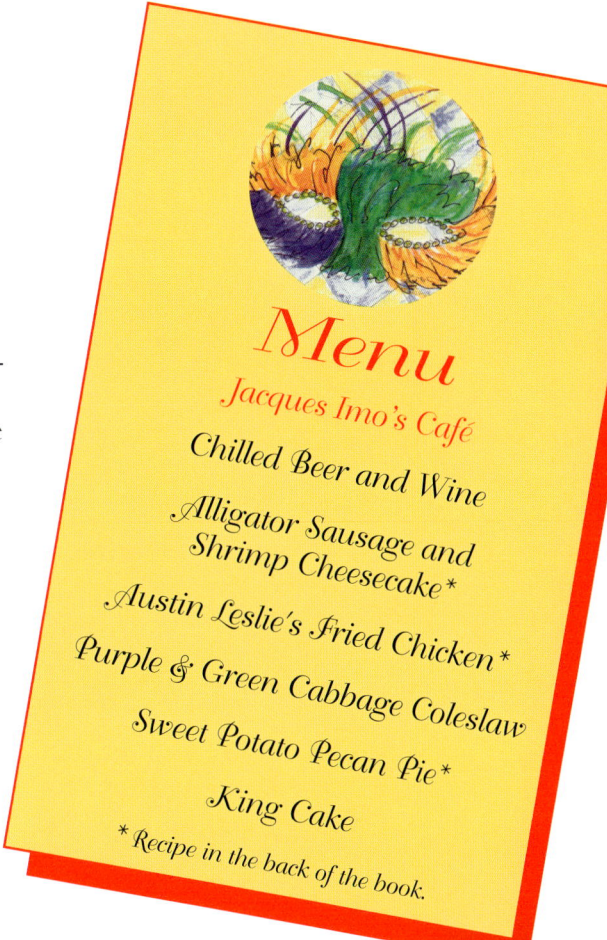

…le set for royalty – and revelry.

Menu
Jacques Imo's Café

Chilled Beer and Wine

Alligator Sausage and Shrimp Cheesecake*

Austin Leslie's Fried Chicken*

Purple & Green Cabbage Coleslaw

Sweet Potato Pecan Pie*

King Cake

* Recipe in the back of the book.

What to Pack:

- 1 purple, green and gold feather boa
- A whole heap of Mardi Gras beads
- A dozen or more paper crowns
- A dozen or more Mardi Gras masks
- 2 fabulous faux crowns, scepters and capes for the king and queen
- Mardi Gras music, CDs or tapes
- 3 green Celebration holders
- Faux flowers in purple, gold and green
- Gold-stamped napkins
- 6 satin favor bags (for the gentlemen) filled with small gifts, such as soaps, candies or note cards.

The Moveable Mardi Gras Suitcase is packed and ready to go.

Flair for the Affair

- Play Mardi Gras music including "Mardi Gras in New Orleans-Volume II" by The Meters and Bill Lagman "Mobile's Mardi Gras Music Man."
- Follow the custom used at New Orleans Carnival balls wherein ladies receive a small favor from their partner after each dance.
- Order a classic king cake.
- Give a fun prize to the person that gets the baby in the king cake.

Décor and More

- Gold stamped napkins
- Feather boa and beads
- Paper crowns and masks
- Celebration holders with faux flowers

Invitation Ideas

- A gold paper crown with the invitation written on it.
- A small cake box with beads, doubloons and invite inside, all tied up with purple, green and gold ribbon.
- Invitation attached to a mask.

Carnival colored beads, Mardi Gras music, picture frames, favor bags and authentic King Cake dolls are among the take-along essentials.

A Mardi Gras mask doubles as a napkin ring.

How To

Gold Stamped Napkins

Buy a dozen 20" x 20" cloth or linen napkins. Lay the napkins flat on newspaper. Paint the desired stamp (we used a bee, but a crown or fleur de lis also work well) with a thin layer of gold fabric paint and stamp onto fabric. Lift, paint and stamp again in another spot until the designs covered the napkin as desired. When the paint is dry, heat set according to the paint directions in the dryer. (Stamps and fabric paint can be purchased at a craft store.)

King Cake

King cakes can be ordered from Randazzo's King Cake Express (504) 279-1834 or www.kingcakeexpress.com.

Feather Boas, Beads, Crowns, Scepters, Masks and Music

May be ordered from Accent Annex Mardi Gras headquarters in New Orleans (504) 733-4700, or Toomey's Mardi Gras in Mobile (877) 450-5077.

Celebration Holder with Faux Flower

Simply add faux flowers in Carnival colors to the Celebration holders. (See catalogue in the back of book to order celebration holders.)

Celebration vases by Bev Church with Luis Colmenares hold feather flowers that are easy to pack.

Cabaret/Milestone Birthday

The Party Plan

A milestone birthday calls for a special celebration. Create a unique theme for the event by concentrating on the talents, hobbies or special interests of the guest of honor. (This party was designed around the interests of Bev's friend, M.I. Scoggin, which include theatre, singing and gardening.) Arrange for guests to meet at an intriguing appointed location for cocktails. (In this case, it was a chic club where M.I. had recently starred in a performance as chanteuse Edith Piaf.) Then everyone travels together to the big birthday bash. There, the guests and the honoree share a sumptuous supper followed by the evening's entertainment. (We crafted up a temporary stage for singing Frank Sinatra and show tunes, cabaret-style.)

Menu
Gautreau's

Chilled Champagne and Pinot Blanc

Peppered Gulf Shrimp with Citrus Gastrique*

Turnip Cream Soup with Truffled Watercress Salad*

Grilled Salmon Roulade*

Lavish Birthday Cake

* Recipe in the back of the book.

Chair accented with large faux marigolds.

...nd-white striped fabric
...ame fashioned out of
...pipe serves as a
...ary stage.

...ious, chocolate doberge
...vered with camellias.

Fanciful, faux flowers accent a garden-themed tablescape.

Flair for the Affair

- Commission an artist to create a fun painting for the guest of honor.
- Showcase everyone's talents on a faux stage.
- Hire a piano player to play requested show tunes for singing and dancing.
- Set up a karaoke machine.
- Encourage each guest to write a special note on their place card to give to the birthday girl (or boy).

Décor and More

- Cabana-striped cabaret stage
- Chairback decorations
- Painted banana leaves
- Banana leaf arrangement in umbrella stand

Invitation Ideas

- Invitation designed as a Playbill.
- A small birthday cake in a pretty box (4"x 4"x 4") tied with a ribbon and a card attached with party particulars.

A hand-painted sign beckons the birthday girl and guests to come to the cabaret. Sign painted by Dr. Bob.

Painted metal banana leaves feature the honoree's interest in gardening. Leaves painted by Karin Rittvo.

How To

Make a Stage

Cover the holes in the bottoms of two large pots (14-inches in diameter) using cling tape. Fill each pot half-full with sand. Insert a 10 foot piece of plastic PVC pipe (1 $1/2$ inch diameter) into each pot. Add additional sand to completely fill each pot. Attach a 6 foot piece of plastic PVC across the top with two plastic connectors. Drape a piece of fabric 45 inches wide by 8 feet in length across the top (with approximately one foot of fabric at each end). Gather the fabric together at each end and tie to achieve a graceful swoop in the center. Then, take two additional pieces of fabric, each 22 feet by 45 inches wide (or whatever the width of desired fabric), and drape over the top so that there is an equal amount of fabric in the front and back. Be sure to completely cover the tied ends of the fabric on the corners. Tuck under the bottom edges of the fabric to make a pretty puddle on the floor.

Banana Leaf Arrangement in Umbrella Stand

Place the base of a pool umbrella on the table. Add painted metal banana leaves, then large faux flowers. Wrap the stand with tulle to cover.

Painted Banana Leaves

We found metal banana leaves at Pier-1 Imports. Sand the leaves lightly, then coat with rust resistant paint. Paint with desired designs and finish with clear polyurethane.

Gallery Opening Gala

104

The Party Plan

Winter often features a flurry of gallery openings and art showings. Take advantage of these events by inviting 8 to 10 friends to join you for an art-filled evening. Start the festivities with wine and incredible appetizers, then with a warming, wonderful meal featuring favorite comfort foods. Then everyone heads out, bedecked in billowy feather boas, to paint the town red during a night of gallery hopping. Take a limousine to ensure a safe expedition and a showy arrival at each stop along the way. Upon your return, offer a decadent dessert for the finale.

Menu
Dooky Chase

Chardonnay and Beaujolais

Cheese Straws

Broccoli Salad with Walnuts*

Roasted Hen with Dried Fruit and Raisin Sauce*

Garlic Mashed Potatoes*

Bailey's Irish Cream Custard Cake*

Recipe in the back of the book.

The cake centerpiece filled with sunflowers, Gerbera daisies and asters.

...naginative, art-filled tablescape ...owing with color and creativity.

A hand-painted sign hung from a boa-draped chair sets the tone for the event.

105

Flair for the Affair

- Have all the ladies wear matching feather boas.
- Hire a limousine or van to take everyone gallery hopping.
- Take along a couple of decorated umbrellas in case of inclement weather (or simply to second-line).

Décor and More

- Decorated umbrellas
- Flower-edged tablecloth
- Flower capped cake
- Flower-filled shoes

Invitation Ideas

- Small painted canvas with invitation painted on it or tied to it.
- A paint brush tied to a colorful invitation.
- A small paint can filled with flowers, write the invitation on paper and glue to the can as the label.

The cake topped with a plethora of posies.

A trio of paintings from Karen Laborde's "Cardio II" series. A metal flower container designed by Bev Church with Julia Yerkov holds a fern frond and a small flower.

How To

Flowers on umbrella.

Decorated Umbrellas

Hot glue faux flowers to the top and the ends of the spines, of an inexpensive umbrella. Then, tack the flowers with thread to secure.

The dramatic midnight blue table overlay edged in faux flowers.

Flower-Edged Tablecloth

Cut fabric to fit your table. Turn under any edges that are not selvage edges and hem to prevent fraying. Take dozens of your favorite faux flowers and disassemble the flowers. Pull the layers of petals off until only one layer remains. (We used roses, zinnias, hydrangeas and lime green snowball viburnum.) Hot glue the green silk leaves from the flowers around the entire edge of the cloth, using wax paper as a drop cloth. Then glue down the single layer flowers and any petals, alternating colors and flowers as you go.

Shoes brimming with flowers serve as a whimsical table accent.

Flower-Filled Shoe

Take a supple plastic party cup and trim until it is low enough to fit inside the selected shoe and not be visible. Add water-soaked oasis to the cup and arrange the flowers. Place the container inside the shoe. (Make sure your arrangement drapes over the edges a bit to hide the cup.)

Flower-Capped Cake

Cut the flowers so that the stems are 2 inches long. (We used sunflowers, dahlias, gerbera daisies, asters, lisianthus, marigolds and other flowers.) Insert the flowers into an already iced cake. Remove the flowers before serving. This cake is not to be eaten. It is a centerpiece.

|107

Spring

Easter Brunch Menu

Commander's Palace

Freshly Squeezed Orange Juice

*Brandy Milk Punch**

*Eggs Sardou**

*Shrimp Cognac and Andouille Stone Ground Grits**

*Buttermilk Biscuits with Strawberries and Sweet Cream**

Commander's Palace
1403 Washington Avenue
New Orleans, LA 70130
Telephone: 504.899.8221
www.commanderspalace.com

Since 1880, Commander's Palace has been a New Orleans landmark known for the award-winning quality of its food and service. Brimming with the Brennan family's gracious Crescent City hospitality, Commander's Palace excels at making dining a special event. Commander's Palace was ranked New Orleans' most popular dining destination for a record 17th straight year in the 2004 Zagat Survey and chosen by the James Beard Foundation for the Outstanding Restaurant Award.
Cookbook: Commanders' Kitchen
by Ti Adelaide Martin & Jamie Shannon

BRANDY MILK PUNCH

Ingredients:
1 1/2 cups milk
1/2 cup heavy cream
12 ounces brandy or bourbon
1/2 cup sugar
1/2 cup very cold water
1 tablespoon vanilla extract
Nutmeg to taste

Preparation:
Combine the milk, cream, brandy or bourbon, sugar, water and vanilla in a large pitcher. Shake well. Serve each cocktail with a sprinkle of nutmeg. Serves 6.

EGGS SARDOU

Ingredients:
2 pounds fresh spinach
1/2 stick or 4 tablespoons butter
1/4 cup flour
1 cup heavy cream
1 teaspoon nutmeg
salt and pepper, to taste
16 medium to large artichokes
2 lemons
1/4 cup whole black peppercorns
16 poached eggs
2 cups hollandaise sauce

Preparation:
Clean spinach, discarding any large stems and brown leaves. Wash spinach in cold water 3 times and tear into 3-inch pieces. Let drain and set aside.

In a large pot over medium heat, melt butter (about 2 minutes). Slowly add flour, stirring constantly with a wooden spoon; cook for about 2 minutes or until roux is pale and has the consistency of wet sand. Stir in cream, nutmeg and season. Simmer for about 2 minutes, stirring constantly until smooth. Add half of the spinach and stir. Cook for about 3 minutes. Add remaining spinach, stir and cook until tender (about 4 to 6 minutes). Adjust seasoning and consistency by adding more cream or cook longer to reduce liquid.

Cut stems off all artichokes. Place artichokes upside down tightly in a large pot, stacking at least two levels high. Slice lemons and add juice and lemons to one quart of water. Add peppercorns and season with salt. Stir and pour over artichokes. Place pot over high heat and cover. Bring to a boil and steam for about 30 to 40 minutes or until done. (When large leaves pull off with little resistance, artichokes are ready.)

When artichokes are done, remove from water and run cold water over them to stop the cooking process, then peel. Scrape out the artichoke with a spoon. Be sure to cut the artichoke bottoms evenly.

To serve, place about a 1/2 cup of cream spinach on center of a hot plate. Place 2 hot artichoke bottoms in center of cream spinach and put poached eggs in the center of each artichoke heart. Spoon about an ounce of hollandaise on each egg. Serves 8.

HOLLANDAISE SAUCE

Ingredients:
1/2 pound butter
4 egg yolks, room temperature
Juice of 1 medium lemon
1 1/2 teaspoons Worcestershire® sauce
Pinch of cayenne pepper
2 tablespoons Chablis or dry Vermouth
Salt, to taste

Preparation:
Melt butter in a skillet over medium heat. Do not let burn. When completely melted, remove from heat.

Put egg yolks, lemon juice, Worcestershire® sauce, and cayenne pepper in top of a double boiler over simmering water. The bottom of the upper pan should not touch the simmering water in the lower pan. Whisk yolks until mixture thickens and forms a sheen, approximately three minutes, no more than five minutes.

In a slow steady stream, add butter, whisking constantly until all butter has been added. Add the wine and whisk well. Sauce should be light and fluffy.

Hold sauce at room temperature until serving time. Makes 2 ½ cups

SHRIMP COGNAC AND ANDOUILLE STONE GROUND GRITS

Ingredients:
2 tablespoons butter
1/2 yellow onion, diced small
1/4 pound Andouille sausage, diced small
1/3 cup yellow stone ground grits
    (We use Anson Mills.)
1/3 cup milk
Kosher salt, to taste
Finely ground black pepper, to taste

Preparation:
Place a medium sauce pot on stove over medium heat. Add butter, onions and sausage to the pan and cook for 5 minutes, or until the onions are translucent. Pour in the milk and bring to a simmer. Slowly whisk in the grits to avoid lumps. Bring the milk back to a boil, turn down the heat to low and continue to slowly simmer, stirring frequently for at least 1 ½ hours or until smooth and creamy. Season with salt and pepper. Keep hot until ready to serve.

Shrimp Ingredients:
2 ounces clarified butter
2 tablespoons minced garlic
1 cup leeks, cut into 1/4-inch half-moons
    and rinsed very well
1 pound fresh Gulf shrimp, peeled and
    deveined
1 tablespoon Creole seasoning
2 cups chopped forest mushrooms
    (chanterelles, morels and oyster mushrooms)
1 cup tomatoes, peeled, deseeded and
    diced small
4 ounces Hennessy Cognac (or your favorite)
4 ounces reduced shrimp stock
3 ounces veal stock
3 tablespoons butter
2 tablespoons chopped fresh thyme
Kosher salt and freshly ground black
    pepper, to taste

Preparation:
Place a large sauté pan on the stove over high heat. Add the clarified butter and the garlic and stir constantly until golden brown. Add the leeks and stir and cook for 1 minute. Add the mushrooms and tomatoes and continue to sauté for 3 minutes. Remove the pan from the stove and add cognac. Flame and continue to cook for 1 minute. Add the shrimp stock and veal stock and reduce to sauce consistency and add shrimp. Add the thyme and slowly add in the butter, then season with salt and pepper. Serve over grits.

Place the grits into the center of a hot bowl and spoon the shrimp mixture over the top. You may choose to garnish with slivered green onions and a sprig of thyme. Serves 4.

COMMANDER'S BUTTERMILK BISCUITS WITH PONCHATOULA STRAWBERRIES AND SWEET CREAM

Biscuits Ingredients:
3 cups all purpose flour
1/2 teaspoon salt
3 teaspoons baking powder
3 teaspoons sugar
16 tablespoons cold, unsalted butter,
    cut into 1-inch cubes
1 ½ cups buttermilk
Powdered sugar, for dusting

Strawberries Ingredients:
3 pints ripe strawberries (smaller berries are
    generally the sweetest)
2 to 3 cups
    of the berries

Whipped Cream 1.
3/4 cup heavy cream,
1/4 cup sugar

Preparation:
First, make the biscuits. Preheat oven to degrees. Sift together the flour, salt, baking p der, and sugar in a large bowl. Gently cut in the butter, taking care not to break up the butter too much. Form a well in the center of the mixture, add the buttermilk, and lightly fold the mixture so that it's just sticky and the dry ingredients just moistened. Do not overwork the dough; the less you handle it, the flakier the biscuits will be.

On a surface, lightly dusted with flour, flatten the dough to 1 ½-inch thickness. Using a flour-dusted cutter 3 inches in diameter, cut the dough into biscuit shapes and set the biscuits touching each other in a pie tin so that they stay moist while they bake. Bake biscuits for 20 minutes. Do not over bake.

To prepare the strawberries, wash them and cut them in half; if they are large, cut them in quarters. One hour before serving, combine the berries and the sugar. The sugar mixture should be of a syrup-like consistency.

To prepare the whipped cream, place the chilled heavy cream and sugar in a bowl and whip with a whisk or an electric mixer. When the cream thickens, add the sugar. Do not over whip. The biscuits should be served warm but should have cooled enough to prevent the whipped cream from melting.

To assemble, cut the biscuits in half horizontally, and dust the top halves with powdered sugar. Place the bottom half of each biscuit on a dessert plate and top each with a portion of the strawberry mixture and an appropriate amount of syrup. Top with a dollop of the whipped cream. Top each with a sugared biscuit top. Serves 6.

Galatoire's

Wines from Provence

Oyster Pan Roast*

Chicken Bonne Femme*

Bread Pudding with Banana Sauce*

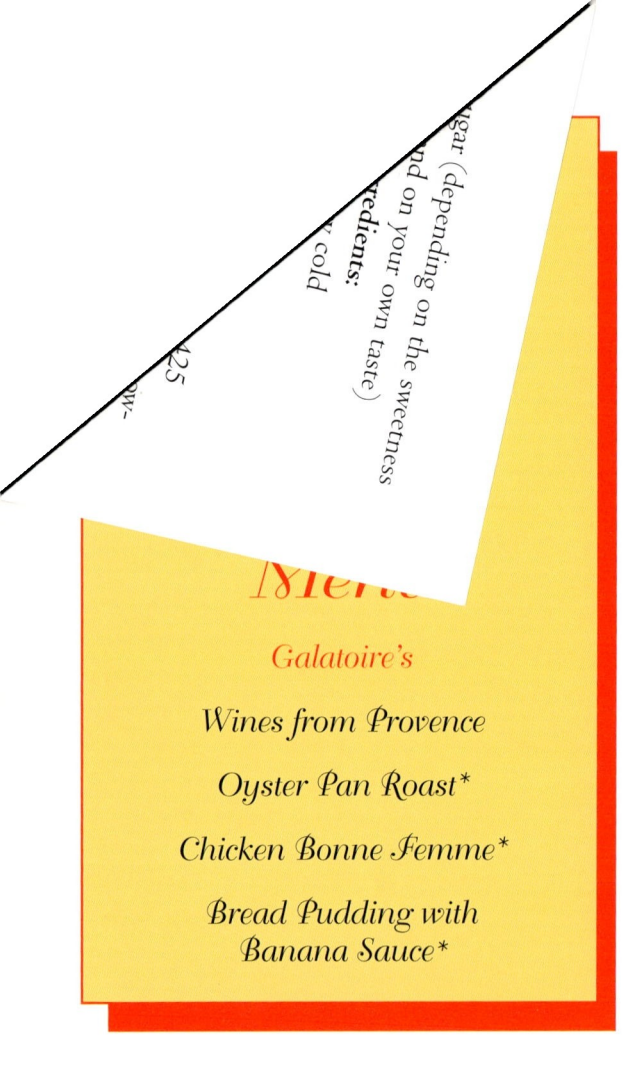

Galatoire's
209 Bourbon Street
New Orleans, LA 70130
Telephone: 504.525.2021
www.galatoires.com

Galatoire's Restaurant, located on Bourbon Street in New Orleans, has been a landmark since 1905. It has been owned and operated by family members for five generations and prides itself on serving consistently top-quality classic French Creole cuisine. Galatoire's offers an elegant familial dining experience along with a daily menu that has remained much the same since the restaurant opened. Oyster's Rockefeller, Creole gumbo, Oysters en Brochette, Crabmeat Maison, Trout Meuniere... are some of Galatoire's timeless specialties.

Oyster Pan Roast

Ingredients:
1 tablespoon butter
1 cup yellow onion, finely diced
1/2 cup shallots, finely diced
1/4 cup green onions, finely chopped
36 large Gulf oysters
3 tablespoons chopped garlic
1/2 cup white wine
1 cup heavy cream
1/2 cup grated Parmesan cheese
Salt
White pepper
1 cup seasoned breadcrumbs
1/2 cup clarified butter

Preparation:
Melt butter in a sauté pan over high heat. Sauté yellow onions, shallots and green onions until translucent, approximately 3 minutes. Add the oysters and sauté over high heat until the edges start to curl slightly, approximately one minute. Add garlic and sauté for one minute more. Add white wine, swirl the pan to de-glaze and allow to simmer for 2 minutes. Add heavy cream and simmer until sauce begins to reduce, approximately 4 minutes. Add Parmesan cheese and season with salt and pepper to taste. Heat broiler. Evenly divide the oysters and sauce into 6 individual portion-sized casserole dishes. The oysters should not be fully submerged beneath the sauce. Sprinkle with breadcrumbs, drizzle with clarified butter and broil until golden. Serve immediately. Serves 6.

Chicken Bonne Femme

Ingredients:
2 chickens, cut up for frying
1/2 cup oil
4 potatoes sliced thin
1 large onion, sliced thin
1 clove garlic, minced
Salt and pepper, to taste
Parmesan cheese, to taste
1 tablespoon minced fresh parsley

Preparation:
Sauté chicken in oil to desired degree of doneness. While chicken is frying, cottage fry the potatoes. After chicken is browned but not entirely done, add onion, garlic, salt and pepper to taste. Before serving, drain all oil from chicken and top with potatoes, Parmesan cheese and parsley. Serves 4.

Bread Pudding with Banana Sauce

Ingredients:
11 eggs
1 1/3 cups sugar
1 quart whole milk
1 teaspoon vanilla extract
1 teaspoon ground cinnamon
French bread, cut into 2 dozen 3/4-inch slices

Preparation:

Preheat oven to 350 degrees. In a large mixing bowl, combine eggs, sugar, milk, vanilla, and cinnamon and whisk until well blended. In a non-stick oversized muffin pan, for 12, place two slices of the bread into each muffin hole. Pour the egg and milk mixture into each muffin hole. Allow the bread to absorb the mixture and repeat the process until the bread is saturated and the muffin hole is full (it may take 3 or 4 fillings to totally saturate the bread and fill the hole). Bake the pudding mixture for 35 minutes or until the pudding has turned golden and set in the pan. When the pudding is finished, remove from the oven and allow it to sit for about 15 minutes. Invert the muffin pan to remove the puddings. Place each on the center of a plate and ladle banana sauce onto the pudding. Serves 12.

BANANA SAUCE:
Ingredients:
1 pound salted butter
1 pound light brown sugar
4 bananas
1/2 cup praline liqueur

Preparation:
Melt butter in a 2-quart saucepot over medium heat. Add the light brown sugar to the melted butter whisking over the heat until smooth. Slice the bananas and add to the sauce. Lastly, add the praline liqueur to the sauce and keep warm.

Flower Power Menu
Ford Church-Cottonwood Institute

*Cranberry Sparkle**

*Organic Peppermint Tea and Apple Juice**

*Perfect Pizza Pita Pockets**

Cupcakes

*World Famous Organic Banana Bread**

*Mississippi Mud Brownies**

Ford Reese Church
Telephone: 303.447.1076

Ford Church is a native New Orleanian with a passion for good food and the great outdoors. He is the founder and director of the Cottonwood Institute, a nonprofit organization that is dedicated to developing innovative educational programs that blend adventure and service to transform the way students connect with their community. For more info about the Cottonwood Institute, call 303-447-1076 or visit: www.cottonwoodinstitute.org

---

CRANBERRY SPARKLE
Ingredients:
cranberry juice
soda

Preparation:
Fill tall glasses 3/4 full with iced cranberry juice then add purified soda water and a slice of organic lime to each glass.

ORGANIC PEPPERMINT TEA AND APPLE JUICE
Prepare a batch of organic peppermint iced tea and serve in a tall glasses filled with 1/2 peppermint tea and half organic apple juice.

PERFECT PITA PIZZA POCKETS
Ingredients: *(Organic ingredients preferred)*
stone-ground wheat pita bread
pizza sauce
mozzarella cheese
olive oil
mild to wild pizza toppings such as pepperoni, spinach, feta cheese, olives, etc.

Preparation:
Preheat oven to 350 degrees. Grease a baking sheet with olive oil. Cut pita bread in half, open it slightly and slather the inside of the pita pocket with pizza sauce. Add cheese, mild to wild pizza toppings, and baste outside of pita with olive oil. Bake for 10 to 15 minutes or until cheese is melted, the contents are heated, and the outside of the pita is crisp.

Preparation:
Preheat oven to 350 degrees. Grease bread pans with butter. In a large mixing bowl, add dry ingredients. Then mash bananas and slowly add wet ingredients. Mix thoroughly by hand and pour contents into greased bread pans. Bake for 1 hour or until knife can be inserted and removed from center of loaf without batter. Makes 2 loaves.

Preparation:
Melt the 2 sticks of butter in a medium saucepan and add the 4 ounces of chocolate. Cook on low until melted. Cool. Add flour, sugar and salt and beat the eggs into the mixture. Add vanilla and mix well. Pour into a 9-inch x 12-inch baking pan. Cook at 350 degrees for 20 to 25 minutes. Remove from oven. While brownies are still hot, sprinkle the marshmallows and pecans all over the top. Melt butter and chocolate. Add confectioner's sugar a little at a time alternating with the half and half. Beat and cook on low until smooth. Remove from heat and stir in vanilla. Pour the hot mixture evenly over the marshmallows and pecans. Makes approximately 2 dozen brownies.

WORLD FAMOUS ORGANIC BANANA BREAD
Ingredients: (Organic Ingredients Preferred)
4 cups stone-ground wheat flour
2 teaspoons baking powder
1 teaspoon sea salt
2 teaspoons cinnamon
1/2 teaspoon nutmeg
1 cup salted butter
2 cups raw unbleached cane sugar
4 hormone-free, free-range eggs
4 ripe free-trade bananas
1 cup chopped walnuts or pecans
2 teaspoons vanilla
2 cups hormone-free milk

MISSISSIPPI MUD BROWNIES
Brownie Ingredients:
2 sticks butter
4 ounces unsweetened chocolate
2 cups sugar
1 1/2 cups flour
4 eggs
1/4 teaspoon salt
1 teaspoon vanilla

Topping Ingredients:
1 (10 ounce) package of mini marshmallows
1 1/2 cups chopped pecans
1 box confectioner's sugar
1 stick butter
2 ounces unsweetened chocolate
1 teaspoon vanilla
6 tablespoons half and half

Graduation Party Menu

Ralph's on the Park

White Wine
Iced Tea

Jalapeño Shrimp with Spiced Corn Salsa on Tomato Pinwheels*

Lemon Herb Chicken

Lentil, Barley and Rice Salad*

Bete Noire with White Chocolate Drambuie Sauce*

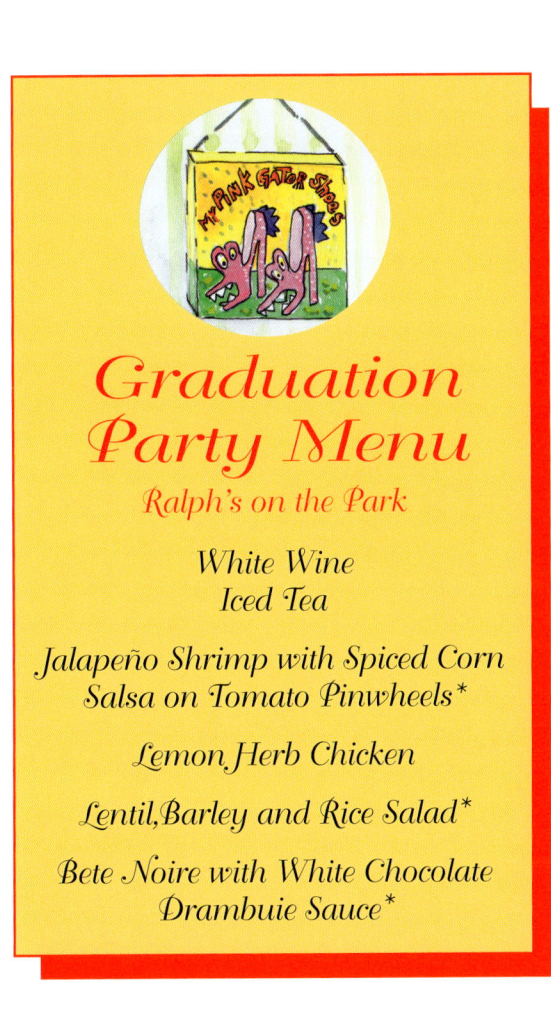

Ralph's on the Park
900 City Park Avenue
New Orleans, LA 70119
Telephone: 504.488.1000
www.ralphsonthepark.com

Ralph's on the Park is located in a glorious, historic building (circa 1860), overlooking New Orleans' beautiful City Park. In January 2003, restaurateur Ralph Brennan teamed up with chef Gerard Maras, of Mr. B's and Gerard's Downtown fame, and Richard Shakespeare, a twenty-five year Commander's Palace management veteran to open this new eatery "For Locals, By Locals" in this historic culinary location.

Jalapeño Shrimp with Spiced Corn Salsa on Tomatoes

Shrimp Boil:
3 1/2 quarts water
4 tablespoons kosher salt
6 whole jalapeños, chopped with seeds
3 ounces fresh ginger, peeled and chopped
6 whole bay leaves
1 whole garlic bulb, cut in half
1 whole orange, zest only (juice reserved)
1 whole lime, zest and juice
1 teaspoon crushed red pepper
4 to 5 pounds shrimp (approximately 100)

Preparation:
Combine all ingredients for the shrimp boil, except shrimp, into a stainless-steel sauce pot. Bring to a boil, then simmer for 25 minutes. Strain shrimp boil thru a chinois. Return strained liquid to a boil, add shrimp. When liquid once again returns to a boil, reduce to a simmer. Cook shrimp for 2 minutes, then remove from heat. Let shrimp remain in boil additional 3 to 4 minutes, then drain. Lay shrimp out on a sheet pan and refrigerate to cool completely.

Note: The shrimp boil can be used twice to boil additional shrimp.

Spiced Corn Salsa

Ingredients:
3 whole jalapeño peppers, diced
1 cup diced red bell pepper
6 ears Silver Queen corn, kernels removed, cobs scraped
1/3 cup chopped parsley
1/2 cup green onion, white part only, sliced thin greens
1 teaspoon chopped garlic
1 1/4 cups olive oil
1 1/4 cup lime juice and zest
1/4 cup orange juice and 1/2 zest
1/4 cup lemon juice and 1/2 zest
1 teaspoon kosher salt
2 teaspoons minced ginger
Boiled shrimp
4 large Creole tomatoes

Preparation:
In a stainless-steel bowl, whisk together all ingredients except the peppers, onions and corn. Taste for seasoning, then add remaining ingredients including shrimp. Make salsa at least 2 to 3 hours before serving to allow the jalapeño and ginger flavor to emerge. Keep bowl on ice bath until ready to serve.

To serve, cut slices of a Creole tomato into 1/2-inch slices, then cut each slice in half. In the center of each plate, arrange tomato halves in a pinwheel configuration. Spoon salsa with 8 or so shrimp onto the tomatoes on each plate. Sprinkle with sliced green onion and chiffonade of parsley. Garnish each with a small sprig of frisee lettuce and a small wedge of lime. Serves 12.

*Note: Serve very cold on a chilled plate.

Lentil, Barley and Rice Salad

Ingredients:
1 cup pearled barley
1 cup basmati rice
1 cup red lentils
1 cup green lentils
1/2 cup white balsamic vinegar
1/2 cup extra virgin olive oil
12 ounces red onion, minced
3/4 cup pine nuts, toasted
3/4 cup golden raisins
1/4 cup Italian parsley, chopped
1/3 cup chiffonade of mint

1/2 teaspoon fresh ground black pepper
1 teaspoon kosher salt
Juice of 1 lemon

Preparation:
Cook each of the cups of grain independently, in salted water, with a bay leaf added. Be careful to cook all grains slowly, and just before each is finished cooking, remove from heat and allow to set for 5 minutes. Rinse grains quickly, under warm water, just to remove excess starch. Place in a large stainless-steel bowl. Add raisins, onions, pine nuts, herbs along with olive oil, vinegar and lemon juice. Season with salt and pepper. Let salad sit at room temp for 15 minutes, then adjust seasoning as needed. Cover and refrigerate. Serves 12.

Bete Noire with White Chocolate Drambuie Sauce
Ingredients:
8 ounces unsweetened chocolate
4 ounces semi- or bittersweet chocolate
1/2 cup water
1 1/3 cups sugar
1/2 pound unsalted butter, at room temperature in small pieces
5 extra large eggs, at room temp

Preparation:
Preheat oven to 350 degrees with the rack in the center of the oven. Butter a 9-inch cake pan (not a springform) and place a circle of parchment or wax paper on the bottom, covering it completely. Butter the paper. Chop both the chocolates into fine pieces and set aside. Combine the water with 1 cup of the sugar in a heavy 1.5 quart saucepan. Bring to a rapid boil over high heat and cook about 2 minutes. Remove saucepan from the heat and immediately add the chocolate pieces, stirring until they are completely melted. Then add the butter, piece by piece, stirring to melt it completely. Place the eggs and remaining 1/3 cup sugar in either the bowl of an electric mixer or a regular mixing bowl. For a cake with a crunchy crust: beat the eggs and sugar in the electric mixer until they have tripled in volume. For a smooth top (better for frosting): mix the eggs and sugar only until the sugar dissolves.

Add the chocolate/butter mixture to the eggs and mix to incorporate completely. Do not over beat. This causes nasty air bubbles. Spoon and scrape the mixture into the prepared pan. Set the pan into a slightly larger pan or a sturdy jelly roll pan. Set both in the oven and pour hot water into the larger pan. Bake for 25 to 30 minutes. Let cool in the pan for 10 minutes and then run a sharp knife around the sides to release the cake. Cover with plastic wrap and unmold onto a cookie sheet. Invert a serving plate over the cake and flip it over, so the plate is on the bottom and the cake is on the top. Serve with either a chocolate ganache glaze or a white chocolate sauce. Serves 12.

White Chocolate Drambuie Sauce
Ingredients:
9 ounces white chocolate, chopped
1 cup cream
3 ounces Drambuie

Preparation:
In a 1 quart double-boiler sauce pan, heat cream to a boil, add white chocolate, remove from heat, stir to melt chocolate. Add Drambuie, serve at room temperature.

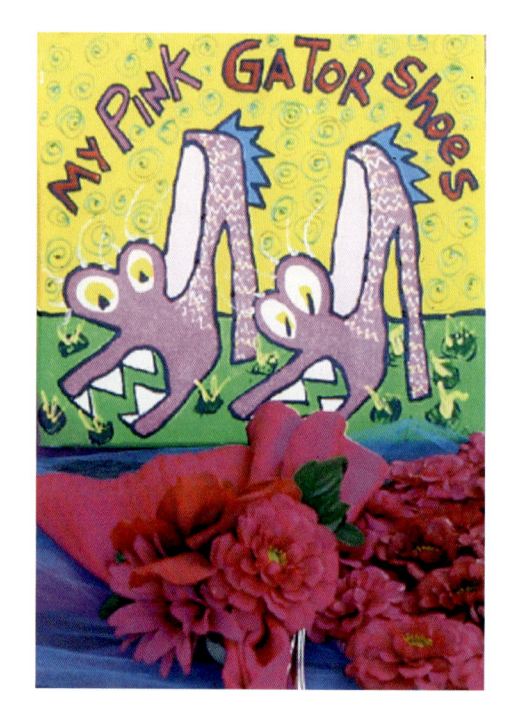

Red-Hot Rose Soirée Menu

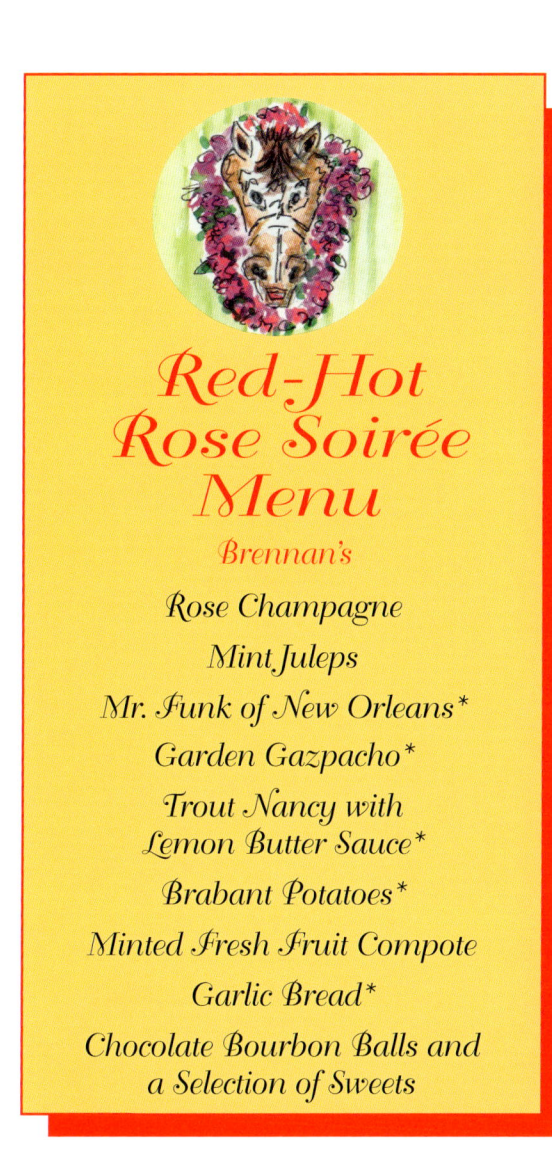

Brennan's

Rose Champagne

Mint Juleps

Mr. Funk of New Orleans*

Garden Gazpacho*

Trout Nancy with Lemon Butter Sauce*

Brabant Potatoes*

Minted Fresh Fruit Compote

Garlic Bread*

Chocolate Bourbon Balls and a Selection of Sweets

Brennan's Restaurant
417 Royal Street New Orleans, LA 70130
Telephone: 504.525.9711
E-Mail: BRENNANSNO@aol.com
www.brennansneworleans.com

Founded by Owen Edward Brennan in 1946, Brennan's is a world-renowned restaurant that has received accolades from the top food critics in the world. The restaurant is located on Royal Street in the famous French Quarter of New Orleans and is housed in an historic 1795 mansion that was built by the great-great grandfather of noted French artist, Edgar Degas.

The 35,000-bottle wine cellar is celebrated as one of the finest and largest of any restaurant in the world. Today, Brennan's is operated by Owen, Jr. ("Pip"), Ted and Jimmy, the sons of the founder. Cookbook: *Breakfast at Brennan's and Dinner, Too* by Pip, Jimmy & Ted Brennen.

Mr. Funk of New Orleans

Ingredients:
3 ounces Champagne
2 1/2 ounces cranberry juice
1/2 ounce peach schnapps
1 whole ripe strawberry

Preparation:
Pour Champagne into a stemmed glass, then add cranberry juice and schnapps. Garnish with a strawberry and serve. Serves 1.

Trout Nancy with Lemon Butter Sauce

Ingredients:
8 trout fillets (Drum, redfish or tilapia can be substituted.)
All-purpose flour for dredging
1/4 cup butter (1/2 stick)
1 1/2 pounds lump crabmeat, picked over to remove any shell or cartilage (blanched crawfish tails can be substituted)
1/2 cup capers
1 1/2 cups lemon butter sauce (see recipe)
Salt and black pepper

Preparation:
Season the trout fillets on both sides with salt and pepper, then dredge in flour. Melt the butter in a large sauté pan and cook the fish over medium heat until flaky, about 4 minutes per side. Remove fish from the pan and place in a warm oven until serving. Cook the crabmeat and capers briefly in the pan drippings until hot. Place a trout fillet on eight plates and top with the crabmeat and capers. Spoon lemon butter sauce over the fish and serve. Serves 8.

Lemon Butter Sauce

Ingredients:
1/2 cup brown sauce (see recipe)
1/4 to 1/2 cup lemon juice
2 pounds butter, room temperature

Preparation:
Combine brown sauce and 1/4 cup of the lemon juice in a large saucepan. Working the pan on and off direct heat, add the butter a bit at a time, whisking the sauce smooth between additions. Add lemon juice according to taste. When all the butter is incorporated, transfer the sauce to another pan or bowl and hold at room temperature until serving. Makes 4 cups.

Brown Sauce
Ingredients:
3 tablespoons butter
3 tablespoons all-purpose flour
1 tablespoon tomato paste
1 tablespoon Worcestershire® sauce
2 tablespoons prepared steak sauce
2 cups beef stock

Preparation:
Melt butter in a large saucepan. Blend in flour, then add remaining ingredients and stir until smooth. Cook over medium heat until the sauce thickens, about 10 to 15 minutes.
Note: Brown sauce can be frozen in 1/2 cup or 1 cup portions for use in numerous recipes.

Brabant Potatoes
Ingredients:
2 large Idaho potatoes, peeled and cubed
1/4 cup butter (1/2 stick)
1 tablespoon garlic, minced
Pinch of paprika
Pinch of salt
1 tablespoon fresh parsley, chopped

Preparation:
Place the potatoes in a large saucepan and add water to cover; boil the potatoes until tender, about 15 to 20 minutes. Drain the potatoes and set aside. Melt butter in a large skillet and sauté the garlic a few minutes over medium heat. Add potatoes, paprika, salt and parsley. Cook briefly, stirring, until potatoes are well coated with the seasonings. Serve hot. Serves 4.

Garlic Bread
Ingredients:
3 small loaves French bread (approximately 12 inches in length)
1/2 cup garlic butter (see recipe)
2 tablespoons paprika
3 tablespoons fresh parsley, finely chopped
1/2 cup Parmesan cheese, freshly grated

Preparation:
Preheat oven to 350 degrees. Split the loaves in half lengthwise. Spread garlic butter onto the cut side of each loaf. Sprinkle with paprika and parsley, then transfer the loaves to a baking sheet. Bake in hot oven for 5 minutes, then sprinkle each slice with Parmesan cheese. Bake an additional 3 minutes and cut each loaf, diagonally, into pieces. Serve warm. Serves 8 to 10.

Garlic Butter
Ingredients:
1/2 cup butter (1 stick), softened
1 teaspoon Worcestershire® sauce
1 tablespoon brandy
3 garlic cloves, minced
1 teaspoon fresh parsley, finely chopped
1 teaspoon Tabasco® sauce
Pinch of salt

Preparation:
Combine all the ingredients together in a small bowl and blend thoroughly. Makes 1/2 cup.

Gazpacho
Ingredients:
2 cups cold beef stock
2 medium cucumbers, peeled, seeded, and finely chopped
1 bunch scallion, finely chopped
1 medium green bell pepper, finely chopped
2 tomatoes, finely chopped
2 garlic cloves, minced
1 cup tomato juice
1 tablespoon red wine vinegar
1/2 teaspoon Tabasco®
Salt and black pepper, to taste
2 teaspoons Worcestershire® sauce
1 teaspoon fresh parsley, finely chopped

Preparation:
Pour beef stock into a large bowl, then add cucumbers, scallions, bell pepper, tomatoes, garlic, tomato juice, red wine vinegar and Tabasco®. Stir until the ingredients are well combined and season with salt and pepper to taste. Chill in the refrigerator for at least 4 hours, then add the Worcestershire® and parsley. Serve the gazpacho in chilled bowls. Serves 6.

116

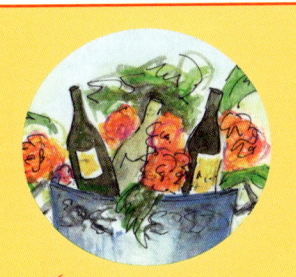

Picnic in the Park Menu

Sallye Irvine - Bay Tables Cookbook

*Bay Cooler Slush**

*Savory Blue Cheesecake with French Bread Rounds**

*Roast Beef Salad with Horseradish Vinaigrette**

Fresh Fruit

S'Mores

Sallye Irvine is a freelance journalist specializing in food, wine and entertaining. Her columns and articles appear regularly in several publications. As an active member of the Junior League, Mrs. Irvine wrote and edited the text of the cookbook, Bay Tables, published by the Junior League of Mobile, Alabama. The following recipes come from Bay Tables.

BAY COOLER SLUSH

Ingredients:
1 (12-ounce) can frozen limeade concentrate
1 (12-ounce) can frozen orange juice concentrate
1 (12-ounce) can frozen pink lemonade
1 (10-ounce) jar maraschino cherries
1 to 2 (12-ounce) cans of rum
3/4 (2-liter) bottle ginger ale

Preparation:
Process the concentrates, undrained cherries, rum and ginger ale in a blender until well blended. Pour into a freezer container. Freeze, covered, until firm. Let stand at room temperature for an hour or two before serving. Serves 8 to 10.

SAVORY BLUE CHEESE CAKE

Ingredients:
1/4 cup fine breadcrumbs
1/3 cup Parmesan cheese, finely grated
8 ounces bacon
1 Vidalia or white onion, minced
24 ounces cream cheese, softened
4 eggs
1/2 cup heavy cream
12 ounces Gorgonzola, Stilton or Roquefort cheese, crumbled
Salt and white pepper, to taste
Dash of Tabasco® sauce

Preparation:
Coat a buttered 10-inch springform pan with breadcrumbs and Parmesan cheese. Cook bacon in a skillet until crisp-fried and crumbly. Drain bacon, reserving 1 tablespoon bacon dripping. Crumble the bacon and set aside. Sauté the onion in the reserved bacon drippings in the skillet until transparent. Process the cream cheese, eggs and cream in a blender or food processor until well combined. Add the crumbled bacon, onion and Gorgonzola cheese and process well. Add the salt, white pepper and Tabasco® sauce. Process until nearly smooth. Pour into the prepared pan. Bake at 300 degrees for 1 1/2 hours or until the middle springs back when lightly touched. Turn off the oven. Let stand in the oven for 1 hour. Serve with crisp French bread rounds or crackers. Serves 12 to 15.

Preparation:
Combine the garlic, olive oil, vinegar, lemon juice, 2 tablespoons of the parsley, sugar, horseradish, cream, salt and pepper in a blender and blend well. Combine the tomatoes, potatoes, beef, green onions, capers and the remaining parsley in a large bowl and toss to mix well. Add horseradish vinaigrette and toss to coat well. Season with salt and pepper. Mound on a platter lined with romaine lettuce. Garnish with hard-cooked eggs. Serves 8 to 10.

ROAST BEEF SALAD WITH HORSERADISH VINAIGRETTE

Ingredients:
2 cloves garlic, finely chopped
3/4 cup olive oil
1/4 cup white wine vinegar
1/4 cup fresh lemon juice
3 tablespoons chopped fresh parsley
1 teaspoon sugar
1 1/2 tablespoons drained prepared horseradish
2 tablespoons heavy cream
Salt and pepper, to taste
1 pint cherry tomatoes
1 1/2 pounds small red potatoes, boiled, cooled and cut into quarters
1 1/2 pounds cold cooked roast beef or steak, trimmed and julienned
1 cup thinly sliced green onions
2 tablespoons capers
Shredded romaine lettuce
3 hard-cooked eggs, quartered

Summer

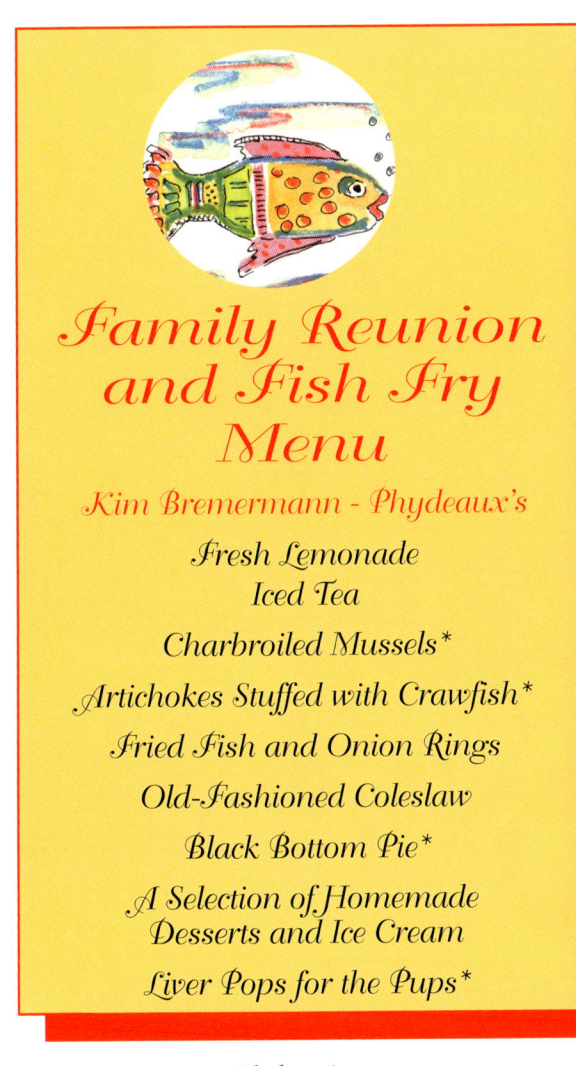

Family Reunion and Fish Fry Menu

Kim Bremermann - Phydeaux's

Fresh Lemonade

Iced Tea

*Charbroiled Mussels**

*Artichokes Stuffed with Crawfish**

Fried Fish and Onion Rings

Old-Fashioned Coleslaw

*Black Bottom Pie**

A Selection of Homemade Desserts and Ice Cream

*Liver Pops for the Pups**

Phydeaux's
505 Jefferson Avenue
New Orleans, LA 70115
Telephone: 504.891.2842

Kim Bremermann loves to cook for her friends. Kim grew up in New Orleans surrounded by the wonderful food and fresh produce that she uses to create her signature dishes.

Her love of animals led her to start her business, Phydeaux's. Phydeaux's is a no-crate dog boarding and day care service. Phydeaux's offers obedience and social skills classes, a pet sitting service and traditional cat boarding.

CHARBROILED MUSSELS

Ingredients:
5 pound bag raw mussels
1 pound butter
1/4 cup garlic, finely chopped
2 tablespoons fresh cilantro, finely chopped
1 cup Parmesan and Romano cheese, grated, (Kim uses Kraft.)

Preparation:
In large pot, steam mussels in about 2 inches of water for about 2 minutes. Mussel shells will just begin to open. Remove from heat immediately. Open mussels and discard half of the shell, leaving the meat on the remaining shell half. Lay them out on a cookie sheet. Mussels are much smaller that oysters so you may want to put 2 or 3 mussels into each shell. Melt butter and sauté garlic and cilantro in sauce pan.

Over high heat, place mussels directly onto the grill. Spoon some of the melted butter mixture onto the mussels. Be careful, when the mixture spills over, the flames will flare up. Add a pinch of the Parmesan/Romano cheese. Grill 3 to 4 minutes until hot and bubbly and the cheese has browned and crusted. Serve immediately.

ARTICHOKES STUFFED WITH CRAWFISH

Ingredients:
4 artichokes (very firm and fat with leaves)
2 tablespoons salt
2 lemons
6 tablespoons garlic, finely chopped
6 tablespoons French shallots, coarsely chopped (not green onions)
4 tablespoons extra virgin olive oil
4 tablespoons butter
2 pounds crawfish tails
4 tablespoons Lea & Perrin's White Wine Worcestershire® Sauce
1 teaspoon Tabasco®
1 teaspoon black pepper
3 teaspoons drained capers (optional)
2 packets Knorr Lemon Herb Cream Sauce mix
2 cups water
1 cup milk
1/2 cup butter
4 to 6 tablespoons mayonnaise

Preparation:
Rinse artichokes well to remove dirt between the leaves. Place in a large deep pot with approximately 2 inches of water, with the salt and lemons (quartered and squeezed over the artichokes). Cover and simmer over medium heat for about 40 minutes or until an outside leaf pulls off easily. Drain and set aside to cool.

In a large saucepan, over medium heat, sauté shallots and garlic in butter and olive oil until lightly browned (2 to 3 minutes). Add crawfish to pan and continue to sauté until crawfish begin to curl and turn deep red (about 2 minutes). Stir in Worcestershire®, Tabasco®, pepper and capers. Remove from heat and set aside.

Prepare the Lemon Herb sauce according to package instructions with water, milk and butter.

Cut artichokes in half lengthwise. Remove thorny center leaves and the fuzzy choke over the heart. Fold mayonnaise into crawfish mixture and spoon a generous amount into the center of each artichoke half. Drizzle Lemon Herb sauce over the artichokes. Serve with a small ramekin of the sauce for dipping. Serves 8 as a side dish, or 4 as an entrée.

Black Bottom Pie

Ingredients:
- 2 dozen Oreo cookies
- 6 tablespoons butter, softened
- 3/4 pound semi-sweet chocolate
- 2 packages vanilla pudding
- 3 cups milk
- 3 egg yolks
- 1 envelope unflavored gelatin
- 1 cup whipping cream

Preparation:
Preheat oven to 300 degrees. Crumble cookies to fine crumbs in a blender or crush in a Ziploc bag. Mix crumbs with butter and press into pie plate. Bake for 15 minutes, remove from oven and set aside to cool. Melt chocolate in microwave oven.

Mix pudding, milk, and egg yolks until blended. Sprinkle gelatin over pudding and cook over low heat, stirring constantly, until mixture is combined and thickened. Fold half of the pudding mixture into the melted chocolate. Spoon the chocolate pudding mixture into the pie shell and refrigerate.

Beat the whipping cream to stiff peaks and fold into remaining pudding mixture. Spoon this mixture over chocolate layer in the pie shell. Decorate with chocolate shavings. Refrigerate until set. Serves 8 to 10.

Liver Pops for the Pups

Ingredients:
- 1/2 pound calf liver

Preparation:
Cut liver into bite sized pieces (appropriate to your dog's size). Spread pieces out on waxed paper and freeze. Once pieces are frozen, you can put them into a plastic container or Ziploc bag. Serve frozen upon request... and they will request them often!

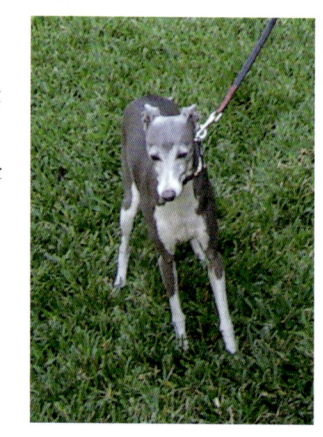

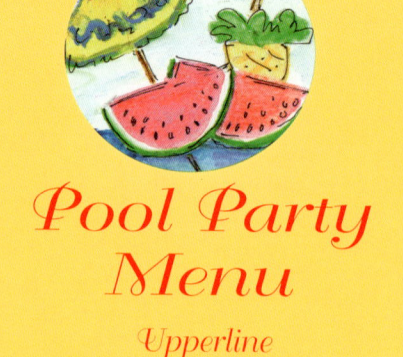

Pool Party Menu

Upperline

Frozen Margaritas
Fruit Smoothies

*Tomato and Onion Salad with Basil Dressing**

*Grilled Fish with Upperline Salad Nicoise**

*Tapenade**

*Cornmeal Poundcake with Summer Berries**

Upperline Restaurant
1413 Upperline Street
New Orleans, LA 70115
Telephone: 504.891.9822
www.upperline.com

The original meaning of the word 'restaurant' was 'to restore' and, says owner JoAnn Clevenger, "Restaurants were originally more than just a place to find a meal; restaurants existed to soothe and bolster the weary soul with comfort and indulgence. Like the earliest restaurants, my goal for the Upperline is to be a haven for our guests, restoring their serenity after the daily hassles of the world with great Louisiana food prepared by Chef Ken Smith, serious wine, and Creole hospitality." sBut Upperline is more than just a restaurant, it is a way of life and a *strong fixture in the local community. From festivals and charity fundraisers, to theme dinners and business etiquette courses for some of New Orleans' most renowned universities. JoAnn has collected a treasure trove of 400 art objects and adds dazzling flower arrangements at the bar. There is always something going on at Upperline.*

Tomato and Onion Salad with Basil Dressing

Ingredients:
Exotic Greens
4 good vine-ripened beefsteak tomatoes (Creole tomatoes if in Louisiana), cut into 1/4-inch slices
2 Vidalia (or Maui Maui or other sweet) onions, sliced thinly

Preparation:
To serve, cover platter with exotic greens. Then alternate layers of tomatoes and onions. Serve with basil dressing.

Basil Dressing

Ingredients:
1 cup fresh basil leaves, well chopped
2 cups homemade mayonnaise
1 tablespoon lemon juice
1 tablespoon Dijon mustard
2 garlic cloves, crushed
Salt and white pepper, to taste

Preparation:
Combine all ingredients in a food processor and taste for salt and pepper.

Upperline Salade Niçoise

Ingredients:
6 new potatoes, sliced
2 cups green beans, halved
1 cup cherry tomatoes, halved
Salt and pepper, to taste
1 cup black calamata olives, pitted and sliced in half
Olive oil or herb vinaigrette, to taste

Preparation:
Cook the potatoes in salted boiling water until just tender.

Cook green beans in heavily salted boiling water for 2 to 3 minutes, drain and refresh in ice water.

Put potatoes, green beans, tomatoes and olives in a bowl and mix with salt and pepper to your taste. At this time, you can add a good olive oil or an herb vinaigrette.

To serve, cover a platter with lettuce leaves and add the Salade Niçoise to the platter. You may top with a grilled fish of your choice.

Grilled Fish

Grill fish in your favorite manner. Red snapper, tuna, salmon and swordfish are favorites of the Upperline.

Tapenade

Ingredients:
2 1/2 cups calamata black olives, pitted
2 anchovies
4 tablespoons capers
1 garlic clove
pinch of cayenne
5 tablespoons olive oil

Preparation:
In the food processor, reduce the olives, anchovies, capers, garlic, cayenne, to a coarse puree. Add the oil and process until the mixture is homogenous.

CORNMEAL POUND CAKE

Ingredients:

2 1/4 cups sifted cake flour

1 1/4 teaspoons baking powder

4 teaspoons salt

3 cups (1 lb.) powdered sugar

4 large eggs, room temperature

1 cup milk, room temperature

8 ounces (2 sticks) unsalted) butter, room temperature

3/4 cup (4 ounces) yellow cornmeal

1/4 cup unsifted powdered sugar

Preparation:
Position rack in lower third of oven; preheat oven to 350 degrees.

Using a paper towel, grease the bottom and sides of the pan with solid shortening. Dust generously with all-purpose flour, shake to distribute and tap out the excess.

Pour flour, baking powder and salt in that order into a triple sifter. Sift onto a sheet of waxed paper, and set aside.

Sift 3 cups of powdered sugar to remove lumps and put on another sheet of waxed paper. Crack eggs into a small bowl, and whisk just to combine the yolks and whites. Pour the milk into a liquid measure cup. Place the butter in the bowl of a heavy duty mixer.

With the flat heater (paddle), cream the butter on medium speed until smooth (about 30 seconds).

Reduce the speed to low, and slowly add the sifted sugar (if the speed is my higher your face will be covered with flying powdered sugar). When all the sugar is added (about 1 minute), stop the machine and scrape the mixture clinging to the sides in to the center of the bowl. Continue to cream on medium until the mixture is light in color and fluffy in texture (3 to 4 minutes).

With the mixer still on medium speed, pour in the eggs, cautiously at first, tablespoon by tablespoon, as if you were adding oil when making mayonnaise. If at any time the mixture appears watery or shiny, stop the flow of eggs and increase the speed until a smooth, silken appearance returns. Then decrease the speed and resume adding eggs.

Continue to cream, scraping the sides of the bowl at least once, or until the mixture appears fluff white, velvety and increased in volume (about 2 to 3 minutes). Detach the beater and bowl from the mixer and tap the beater against the sides of the bowl to free the excess.

Using a rubber spatula, stir in one-forth of the flour mixture. Then add one-third of the milk stirring until blended. Repeat this procedure, alternating dry and liquid ingredients, ending with the final addition of flour. Scrape the sides of the bowl often and mix until smooth after each addition. Stir in the cornmeal just until blended.

Spoon batter into the prepared pan and spread it evenly with the rubber spatula.

Bake for 62 to 67 minutes, or until a toothpick inserted near the center of the cake comes out clean.

(Adding cornmeal to this pound cake provides a delicate crunch to its satiny texture. Makes 12 to 14 servings, with 2 to 3 thin slices per person.)

From *"The Simple Art of Perfect Baking"* by Flo Braker

Upperline chef Ken Smith's note:
Serve with summer fruit: blueberries, blackberries, raspberries and strawberries.

Fourth of July Menu

Mr. B's Bistro

Icy Bottles of Beer & Rootbeer

Spinach, Strawberry & Ricotta Salata Salad*

Honey Ginger Barbequed Pork Chops*

Maque Choux*

Petite Blueberry Cheesecakes

Lemon Pie*

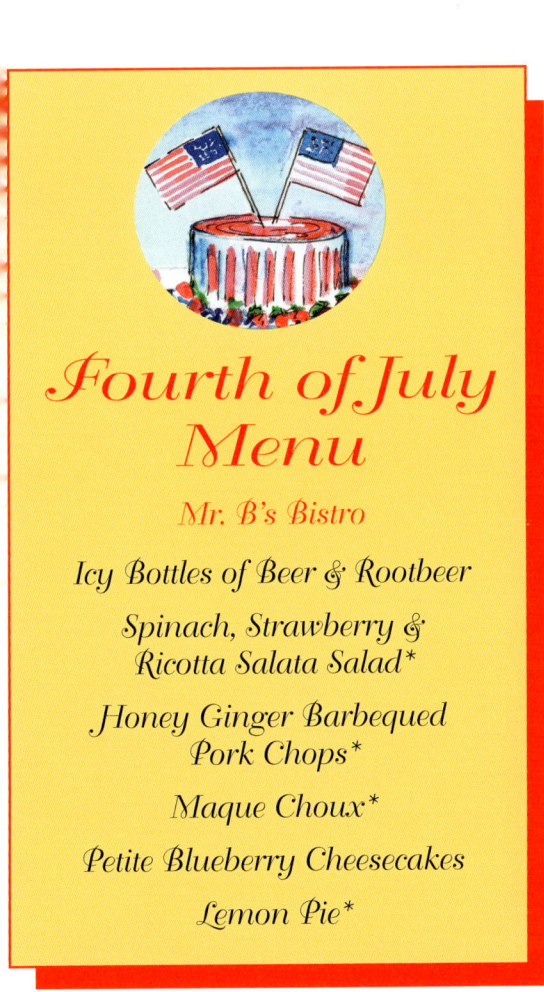

Mr. B's Bistro
201 Royal Street
New Orleans, LA 70130
Telephone: 504.523.2078
www.mrbsbistro.com

Mr. B's is one of the brightest stars in the New Orleans restaurant scene. Cindy Brennan and her famous restaurant family opened Mr. B's in 1979 and it is a true French Quarter fixture famous for deft cooking of regional specialties in a warm bistro setting. Mr. B's has been lauded for their consistently vibrant Louisiana food and impeccable yet friendly service by *Food & Wine, Gourmet, Travel & Leisure* and *Bon Appetit*.

The Mr. B's Bistro Cookbook: Simply Legendary Recipes From New Orleans Favorite French Quarter Restaurant

Spinach, Strawberry, and Ricotta Salata Salad

Ingredients:
2 tablespoons balsamic vinegar
1 teaspoon Dijon mustard
Kosher salt and freshly ground black pepper, to taste
1/4 cup olive oil
8 cups baby spinach (about 1/4 pound)
1/2 cup sliced strawberries
1 ounce ricotta salata cheese

Preparation:
In a bowl whisk together vinegar, mustard, salt, and pepper. Gradually whisk in oil. Add spinach and strawberries, tossing to coat, and season with salt and pepper. With a very sharp knife or a vegetable peeler shave cheese into large shards over salad. Serves 4.

Honey Ginger Barbecued Pork Chop

At Mr. B's we have a smoker, which we use often to smoke a wide range of meats and vegetables. We smoke our pork chops at 60 degrees for 30 minutes before we grill them. If you don't have a smoker at home, just grill them or forgo the grill and sear them on the stove and finish them in the oven. The smoker and the grill impart a pleasant smokiness, but regardless of what cooking method you choose, you'll end up with a great dinner.

Ingredients:
1 cup honey
1/2 cup fresh ginger, finely grated
1/2 cup firmly packed light brown sugar
1/2 cup soy sauce
1/2 cup Asian chili sauce (also known as Siracha)
1/4 cup sesame oil
2 tablespoons minced garlic (about 6 cloves)
1/4 cup minced fresh chives
4 center cut pork chops (each about 3 inches thick and 12 ounces)

Preparation:
Prepare grill. In a bowl whisk together honey, ginger, brown sugar, soy sauce, chili sauce, sesame oil, garlic and chives. Grill chops until a meat thermometer inserted in center registers 155 degrees (time will vary depending on heat of the grill). Serve pork chops drizzled with honey ginger barbecue sauce. Serves 4.

Maque Choux

Ingredients:
2 cups heavy cream
2 tablespoons unsalted butter
1/2 small onion, diced
1/2 red bell pepper, diced
1/2 green bell pepper, diced
3 ears fresh corn, kernels sliced off the cob
Kosher salt and freshly ground black pepper, to taste

Preparation:
In a medium saucepan simmer cream over moderately low heat until it is reduced in half, about 20 minutes. In a large skillet melt butter over moderate heat. Add onion and bell peppers and cook, stirring occasionally, for 3 minutes. Add corn and cook 5 minutes, or until tender. Add reduced cream and cook 1 minute. Season with salt and pepper. Serves 4.

Lemon Pie

Ingredients:
2 cups graham cracker crumbs
3/4 cup melted unsalted butter
1/4 cup firmly packed light brown sugar
2 cups sweetened condensed milk
5 large egg yolks
1/2 cup fresh lemon juice
1 teaspoon lemon zest, freshly grated
1/2 teaspoon vanilla
Whipped cream as garnish

Preparation:
Preheat oven to 350 degrees. In a bowl combine graham cracker crumbs, butter, and sugar and spread into bottom and up sides of a 9-inch pie plate, pressing down. Bake crust in oven 10 minutes. Reduce oven temperature to 300 degrees.

In a bowl whisk together condensed milk, yolks, lemon juice, zest and vanilla. Pour mixture into crust. Bake in oven 20 to 25 minutes, or until set. Makes 1 pie; serves 8.

Caribbean Party Menu

Southern Hospitality Catering

Tropical Rum Punch
Iced Imported Beer

Jerk Chicken with Fried Plantains*

Caribbean Shrimp with Pineapple Rice*

Cuban Beef with Potatoes*

Key Lime Tarts
Chocolate Fountain with Fruit, Marshmallows and Coconut Cookies

---

Southern Hospitality Catering
3259 Chippaewa Street
New Orleans, LA 70115
Telephone: 504.897.0477
Southern Hospitality Catering was established in 1984 by New Orleanian, John Rowland. Since that time, Southern Hospitality has garnered an exceptional reputation, for using the freshest ingredients and displaying extraordinary flair in presentation. Their repertoire includes major events: conventions, weddings, anniversaries... and they cater events in New Orleans and beyond, from California to Maine!

Jerk Chicken with Fried Plantains

Ingredients:
8 (6 ounce) chicken breasts
2 tablespoons olive oil
1 habanera pepper, diced and seeded (use gloves)
4 scallions, chopped
4 sprigs thyme, chopped
2 plantains, peeled and quartered
Salt and pepper, to taste

Marinade Ingredients:
2 medium onions, diced
2 tablespoons garlic, chopped
2 tablespoons fresh ginger, diced
1/2 cup brown sugar
1/2 cup tomato paste
1 teaspoon fresh thyme, chopped
1 teaspoon ground allspice
1/4 cup fresh lime juice (approximately 2 limes)
1 teaspoon ground cinnamon
1/2 cup olive oil
1 red jalapeño pepper, diced and seeded

2 pounds raw shrimp, peeled (50 to 60 count)
1 cup fresh pineapple, diced
1/3 cup fresh basil, chopped
1/2 cup lite soy sauce
1/4 cup green onion, chopped

Preparation:
Cook rice according to directions and set aside to cool to room temperature. In a large skillet, add oils then sauté peppers and yellow onion until lightly brown. Add shrimp and sauté until nearly cooked. Add diced pineapple and fresh basil. Add cooked rice, constantly stirring gently. Add soy sauce and stir until hot. Serve immediately and garnish with chopped green onion. Serves 8.

Preparation:
Marinate chicken overnight. Remove chicken from marinade and discard marinade. In a large skillet, sear chicken breasts until golden brown, finish in oven at 375 degrees until done (approximately 10 to 15 minutes). Remove chicken from pan and set aside. Add habanera, scallions, and thyme to pan. Sauté lightly. Add plantains and brown lightly. Add chicken and simmer until plantain is done, but still firm. Add seasoning. Serve over hot rice. Serves 8.

CARIBBEAN SHRIMP AND PINEAPPLE RICE

Ingredients:
2 cups converted rice, uncooked
1/4 cup sesame oil
1/4 cup olive oil
1 Jalapeño pepper fresh, seeded, diced
1/4 cup dried red bell pepper
1/4 cup onion, diced

CUBAN BEEF WITH POTATOES

Ingredients:
1/4 cup olive oil
1 yellow onion, chopped
1 poblano pepper, chopped
2 pounds beef round, diced into 1-inch cubes
1 tablespoon paprika
1 (16-ounce) can stewed diced tomato
1 tablespoon garlic, minced
1 tablespoon cilantro
1 tablespoon oregano
1 pound Yukon gold potatoes, diced into 1-inch cubes
Salt and pepper, to taste

Preparation:
In a large pan, sauté onion and pepper until light brown. Add beef and paprika and brown. Add tomatoes, garlic, and herbs. Simmer 5 to 10 minutes. Add potatoes and cook until tender. Season to taste. Serve over hot rice. Serves 8.

Biking Bash Menu

Rivershack

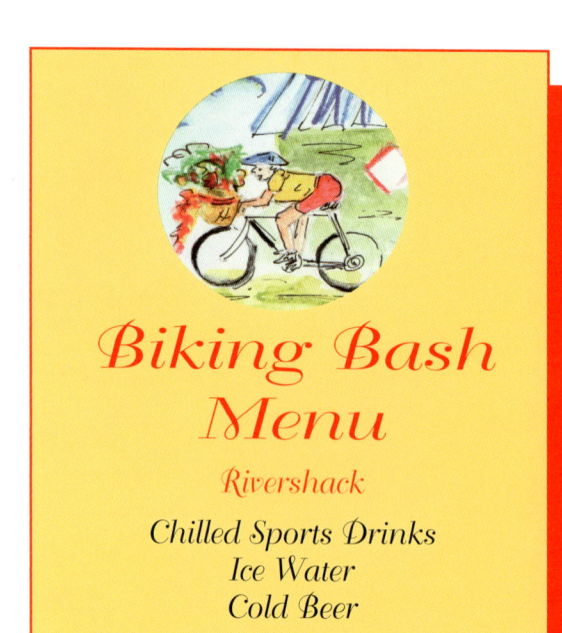

Chilled Sports Drinks
Ice Water
Cold Beer

Blackened Shrimp Remoulade

Fried Green Tomato Salad Napoleon
with Lump Crabmeat*
Herb Vinaigrette Dressing*

Fried Louisiana Quail with Crawfish
and Corn Maque Choux*

Southern Comfort Bread
Pudding with Cassis Cream*

Rivershack Tavern
3449 River Road
Metairie, LA 70121
Telephone: 504.834.4938

The Rivershack Tavern has been characterized as New Orleans' most unusual bar. It is known to have been, at various times, a grocery store, a bar, a restaurant, a package liquor store and a pharmacy. The "Shack" was thrust into the national spotlight when old asbestos shingles were removed from the sides of the 100 year-old building, and underneath, miraculously preserved for over half of a century, were large, vibrantly colored, hand-painted advertisements from the 1940s — in mint condition! Located on historic River Road, adjacent to the Mississippi River, the Rivershack has been described as a cross between a neighborhood tavern, a honky-tonk, a live music club, a sports bar, and a small town restaurant.

Shimmy Shack
1855 Dock Street
New Orleans, LA 70123
504.729.4442
The Shimmy Shack in Harahan, Louisiana is a second fun location opened by the owners of the Rivershack.

Fried Green Tomato Salad Napoleon with Lump Crabmeat

Ingredients:

4 green tomatoes
1 cup flour
2 eggs beaten with 1 tablespoon water to create egg wash
2 cups vegetable oil heated to 350 degrees
8 ounces mixed baby greens
1 pound lump crabmeat
2 ripe avocados
Herb Vinegarette Dressing
Creole seasoning, to taste

Preparation:

Cut green tomatoes into 3/4" to 1" thick slices and dredge in flour. Put into egg wash and back into the flour mixture.

Fry tomatoes in oil heated to 350 degrees, flipping until they are slightly brown on both sides. Drain on a paper towel and set aside. In a separate bowl, put the mixed baby greens, sliced avocado, 3/4 lb. of the crabmeat and toss lightly with the vinegarette and creole seasoning. Put a layer of the greens, avocado and crabmeat mixture on top of a tomato, add another layer of greens mixture and lump crabmeat on the top. Serves 4.

Herb Vinaigrette Dressing

Ingredients:

7 cloves garlic, chopped
2 tablespoons dried thyme or fresh, to taste (fresh is better)
2 tablespoons black pepper or to taste
Creole seasoning, to taste
1 cup Dijon mustard
3/4 cup apple cider
1 1/2 cup olive oil

Preparation:

Mix ingredients in a blender except the oil. Add the olive oil slowly until it emulsifies. This makes 1 quart of dressing and keeps very well in the refrigerator.

Fried Louisiana Quail with Crawfish and Corn Maque Choux

Ingredients:

16 semi boneless quail
Black pepper and cayenne pepper, to taste
1 quart buttermilk
Flour
Creole seasoning, to taste
vegetable oil for frying

Maque Choux Ingredients:
2 large onions, chopped
4 ribs of celery, chopped
2 green peppers, chopped
2 tablespoon garlic, minced
8 ears of corn, kernels cut off cob
4 pounds crawfish tails
1 cup white wine
2 tablespoons flour
2 cups heavy cream
2 bunches green onions, chopped
1 bunch parsley, chopped
4 tablespoons bacon fat
Salt and pepper, to taste

Preparation:
Season quail with black pepper and cayenne pepper then soak in buttermilk overnight.

Sauté onion, celery and bell pepper over medium heat in bacon fat until cooked and almost translucent. Add garlic and corn and sweat for 5 minutes. Add crawfish tails and wine and cook until wine is reduced. Add flour, stir and be careful not to burn. Add cream, cook 3 minutes. Add green onions and parsley. Season with salt and pepper, keep warm.

Dredge quail in flour with Creole seasoning. Heat oil to 350 degrees and fry quail until golden brown. Serve over the crawfish and corn maque choux. Serves 8.

SOUTHERN COMFORT BREAD PUDDING WITH CASSIS CREAM

Ingredients:
6 eggs
1 loaf French bread
1/2 quart cream
2 1/2 cups sugar
1/4 cup vanilla
1/4 cup Southern Comfort

Preparation:
Mix all ingredients together thoroughly and put into greased baking pan. Bake at 325 degrees until stiff, let cool then cut into desired portions. Ladle cassis cream over pudding.

CASSIS CREAM

Ingredients:
1/2 quart cream
1 1/2 cup powered sugar
1/4 cup cassis

Preparation:
Put ingredients into a bowl and whip until thick. Keep refrigerated until ready to use.

Al Fresco Event Menu

Bella Luna, Brennan's and Commander's Palace

White Sangria
Iced Red Zinger Tea

Brennan's Vichyssoise Vieux Carré*

Bella Luna's Creole Crab and Crawfish Cakes with Ancho Aioli *

Commander's Palace Shrimp and Tasso with Five Pepper Jelly*

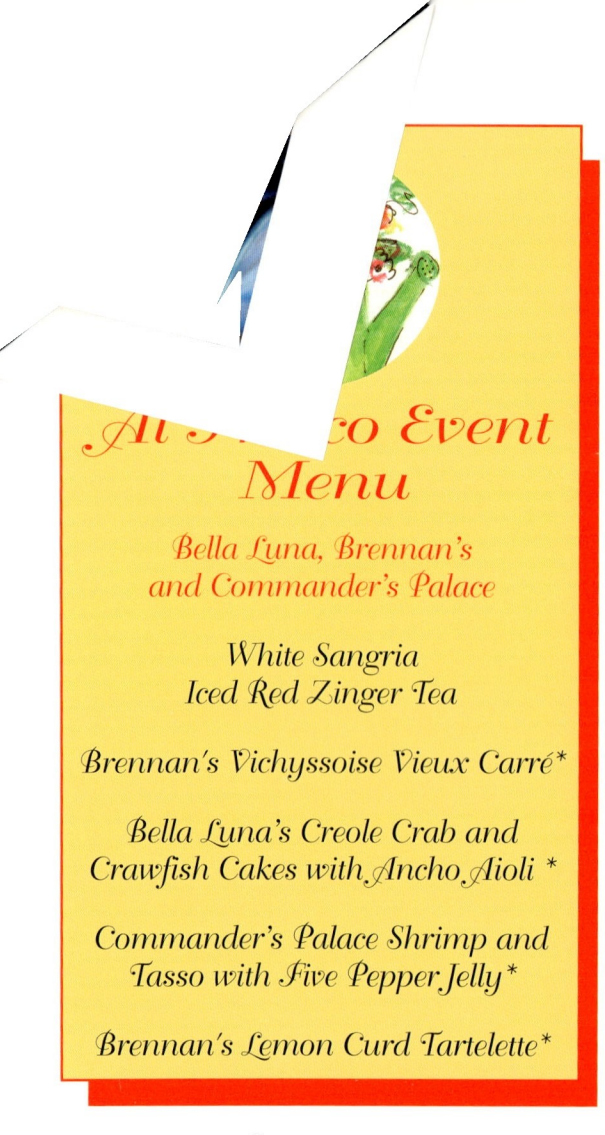

Brennan's Lemon Curd Tartelette*

*Bella Luna Restaurant
See information on page 136*

*Brennan's Restaurant
See information on page 115*

*Commander's Palace
See information on page 108*

BRENNAN'S VICHYSSOISE VIEUX CARRÉ

Ingredients:
5 Large Idaho potatoes, peeled and thinly sliced
3/4 cup diced boiled ham
1 large onion, thinly sliced
1 cup chopped celery
1 cup heavy cream
2 cups milk
1/2 cup chopped shallots
1 tablespoon Worcestershire® sauce
Pinch of cayenne pepper
Pinch of white pepper
Salt to taste
Chopped fresh parsley for garnish

Preparation:
Place the potatoes, ham, onion, and celery in a large pot and add water to cover. Bring the mixture to a boil, then cook over medium heat until the potatoes are very tender, about 20 minutes. Remove the potato mixture from the heat and pour off the excess water. Cream the mixture with a fork or motato masher, then strain in a fine sieve, mashing the potatoes through the strainer. To the strained potatoes, add the cream, milk, shallots, Worcestershire®, and peppers. Adjust the seasonong with salt to taste, then chill for three to four hours.

Serve the vichyssoise in chilled bowls, garnished with chopped parsley. Serves 8 to 10.

BELLA LUNA'S CREOLE CRAB & CRAWFISH CAKES WITH ANCHO AIOLI

Ingredients:
2 stalks celery, finely diced
1 large onion, finely diced
4 cups French bread, cut into 1/4-inch cubes
1/2 pound crab meat, shelled
1/2 green bell pepper, finely diced
1 teaspoon cayenne pepper
2 tablespoons parsley, finely minced
2 cups breadcrumbs
1/2 pound crawfish tails
1/2 red bell pepper, finely diced
2 tablespoons dry mustard
2 tablespoons chives, finely minced
3 egg whites
1/2 cup mayonnaise

Preparation:
Sauté celery and onion in a hot skillet with a little olive oil or butter and then let them cool. After cubing French bread, mix all ingredients together (reserve a small amount of the breadcrumbs for use in forming the cakes). Form crab and crawfish cakes to desired size, and sauté them in skillet with olive oil for 2 to 3 minutes on each side. Serve with Ancho Aioli. Serves 8.

ANCHO AIOLI

Ingredients:
1 red bell pepper
3 ancho peppers
3 chipotle peppers
1 poblano pepper
3 garlic cloves
1 yellow onion
1 bunch green onions
1/2 bunch parsley
1/2 bunch cilantro
1 bunch chives

Preparation:
Roast the above ingredients in hot oil and refrigerate until chilled.

Preparation:
4 tablespoons balsamic vinegar
2 tablespoons dry mustard
2 tablespoons cumin
1 quart mayonnaise
Salt and fresh ground pepper, to taste

Preparation:
In a blender or food processor add the roasted ingredients along with the balsamic vinegar, dry mustard, cumin, mayonnaise, and salt and pepper. Blend until creamy smooth. Serve over crab cakes.

COMMANDER'S PALACE SHRIMP AND TASSO WITH FIVE-PEPPER JELLY

Ingredients:
24 jumbo shrimp, peeled and deveined
1 ounces boneless tasso, julienned in
   1-inch strips
1/2 cup sifted all-purpose flour
Creole Seafood Seasoning to taste
   (see recipe)
1/2 cup vegetable oil
3/4 cup Crystal Hot Sauce Beurre Blanc
   (see recipe)
12 ounces Five-Pepper Jelly (see recipe)
12 pieces pickled okra, cut in half top to bottom

Preparation:
Make a quarter-inch deep incision down the back of each shrimp where it has been deveined, and place one tasso strip in each incision. Secure with a toothpick. Combine the all-purpose flour with Creole Seafood Seasoning, and lightly dust each piece of shrimp with the seasoned flour.

Fry the shrimp in the vegetable oil in a large skillet over medium heat for about 30 seconds on each side. Shrimp should be firm with a nice red-brown color. Remove shrimp and place on a paper towel for a few seconds to drain. Place shrimp in a bowl with Crystal Hot Sauce Beurre Blanc, toss to coat thoroughly, and remove the toothpicks.

Place a portion of Five-Pepper Jelly on each of 8 appetizer plates, and arrange 3 shrimp on the plate alternating with 3 pieces of pickled okra. Serves 8.

FIVE-PEPPER JELLY

Ingredients:
1 1/2 cups light corn syrup
1 1/4 cups cane vinegar (or white vinegar)
1/2 teaspoon red pepper flakes
Salt and freshly ground pepper, to taste
1 each large red, yellow, and green bell pepper, seeded and finely diced
4 jalapeño peppers, seeded and finely diced

Preparation:
Put corn syrup, vinegar, and red pepper flakes in a small saucepan, and season with salt and pepper. Simmer to reduce by two thirds, until mixture is thickened. It will get even thicker as it cools, but the peppers will thin it again when they are added.

Briefly place the peppers in a hot, dry skillet and sauté until tender and their color is brightened, about 30 seconds. Using a slotted spoon, add the peppers to the corn syrup mixture. Makes 2 cups. (Note: This recipe may be made ahead and stored in the refrigerator until ready to use.)

CRYSTAL HOT SAUCE BEURRE BLANC

Ingredients:
1/3 cup Crystal Hot Sauce
   (another hot sauce can be substituted)
2 tablespoons minced shallots
6 medium cloves garlic, peeled and minced
1/4 cup heavy cream
6 tablespoons unsalted butter, softened
Kosher salt, to taste

Preparation:
Place the hot sauce, shallots, garlic and cream in a small saucepan. Over medium heat, simmer until reduced by half, stirring frequently. Remove from heat and slowly whisk in the softened butter, a bit at a time, being careful not to let the sauce break. Strain and keep the sauce warm. Add salt. Makes 3/4 cup.

CREOLE SEAFOOD SEASONING

Ingredients:
1/3 cup salt
1/4 cup granulated or powdered garlic
1/4 cup freshly ground black pepper
2 tablespoons cayenne pepper, or to taste
2 tablespoons dried thyme
2 tablespoon dried basil
2 tablespoons dried oregano

1/3 cup paprika
3 tablespoons granulated or powdered onion

Preparation:
Thoroughly combine all ingredients in a blender, food processor or mixing bowl. Pour the mixture into an airtight container. Will keep indefinitely. Makes about 2 cups.

Brennan's Lemon Curd Tartelette
Ingredients:
1/4 cup grated lemon peel
1/2 cup lemon juice
2 cups sugar
4 large eggs
1 cup (2 sticks) butter
1 cup heavy cream
2 tablespoons powdered sugar
1/2 Teaspoon vanilla
16 small tart shells- purchase the shells or see *Breakfast at Brennan's and Dinner Too* cookbook page 259.

Preparation:
In the top of a double boiler, combine the lemon peel, lemon juice and sugar. Cook the mixture over simmering water until the sugar dissolves, then whisk in the eggs and butter and cook until thick enough to coat the back of a spoon, about five to ten minutes. Transfer the lemon curd to a bowl and cool at room temperature, then refrigerate for 1 to 1 1/2 hours; the curd will thicken as it chills, but not become as thick as pie filling.

In a medium bowl, whip the cream until stiff, then fold in the powdered sugar and vanilla.

Spoon 2 1/2 tablespoons chilled curd into each tart shell and top with the whipped cream. Serves 16.

Autumn

Farmer's Market Menu

Antoine's

Chilled Local or Regional White & Red Wines

Bouillabaisse*

Chateaubriand with Marchand de Vins Sauce Champignons*

Sauté of Fresh Vegetables

Hot Bread

Strawberries with Kirsch*

Antoine's Restaurant
713 St. Louis Street
New Orleans, Louisiana 70130
Telephone: 504.581.4422
Email: info@antoines.com
www.antoines.com

World Famous Antoine's Restaurant is the United States oldest family-run restaurant. Antoine's in the heart of New Orleans French Quarter, opened its doors in 1840 and has had five continuous generations of the Alciatore-Guste family as owners and proprietors. Steeped in tradition, the dining rooms and special party rooms like the Rex Room, the Proteus Room, Escargot Room and the 1840 Room make the Antoine's experience totally unique. Countless celebrities have dined at Antoine's and lining the walls are photographs of the "rich and famous". The wine cellar is legendary with 25,000 bottles of wine with marvelous vintages from the Bordeaux and Burgundy regions of France.
Cookbook: *Antoine's Restaurant Cookbook* by Roy F. Guste, Jr.

Chateaubriand Marchand De Vins Sauce Champignons
Roux Ingredients:
4 tablespoons flour
4 tablespoons butter

Preparation:
In a small heavy skillet melt butter and add the flour. Brown flour until it becomes a dark caramel color and set aside.

Sauce Ingredients:
1 cup white onion, chopped
1 cup mushrooms, chopped
6 cloves garlic, minced
3 tablespoons butter
1 cups beef stock
1 cup red wine
3 tablespoons Lea & Perrins
Salt and pepper, to taste

Preparation:
Sauté onions, mushrooms and garlic with 3 tablespoons of butter until lightly brown. Add the beef stock, wine, Lea & Perrins, and salt and pepper. Cook for 15 minutes, reducing the liquid, add the roux. Mix well. Makes about 3 cups.

Mushrooms Ingredients:
2 pounds sliced mushrooms
4 ounces butter
Salt and pepper, to taste
1 tablespoon parsley, chopped

Preparation:
Sauté mushrooms in butter. Season with salt and pepper, and add the parsley. Simmer 4 to 6 minutes.

Chateaubriand Ingredients:
22-ounce beef tenderloin
1 tablespoon oil
Salt and pepper to taste
1 tablespoon chopped parsley for garnish

Preparation:
Brush the meat with oil and season it with salt and pepper. Cook on a grill or in a heavy iron skillet on all sides to desired doneness. Cut into four medallions.
   Place the sauce to one side of the plate, and the mushrooms on the other side. Put the medallion on the sauce. Sprinkle with chopped parsley. Serves 4.

BOUILLABAISSE

Fish Stock Ingredients:
5 pounds of fish heads and bones (Antoine's prefers red snapper or speckled trout)
1 1/2 medium onion, cut in large slices
1 stalk celery, cut in large slices
3 carrots, cut in large slices
1 bunch parsley, minced
Salt and pepper, to taste
1 1/2 quarts water

Preparation:
Put all ingredients in large soup pot. Simmer until liquid is reduced by half, skimming the top from time to time. Strain stock to remove the bones.

Ingredients:
3 tablespoons butter
1 cup onions, chopped
2 cloves garlic, mashed
2 medium tomato, diced to puree
6 ounces tomato juice
Lemon juice to taste
fish stock
Salt and pepper, to taste
20 shrimp, peeled and deveined
20 oysters
1 teaspoon dried saffron, crushed
4 (5 ounce) fish fillets, browned in skillet or grilled
4 Buster crabs or soft shell crabs, browned in skillet or grilled
Fresh parsley, to garnish

Preparation:
In a large pot, add butter and onions and cook until transparent. Add the garlic, tomatoes, tomato juice, lemon juice and stock. Simmer or reduce for 15 minutes. Add salt and pepper to taste, then add the shrimp, oysters, saffron and cook for 10 to 12 minutes. Add fish and crabs. Simmer for an additional 5 to 8 minutes. Serve with toasted French bread rounds. Garnish with chopped parsley. Serves 4 to 6.

STRAWBERRIES WITH KIRSCH

Ingredients:
3/4 cup strawberries
1/3 cup kirsch
1 tablespoon sugar
Juice from half a lemon

Preparation:
Wash and hull the strawberries. Put them in a small bowl and chill. Pour kirsch over the strawberries and sprinkle with sugar and lemon juice. Toss everything together and mix until the sugar has dissolved. Serve in an ice cream dish. Serves 1.

Blowout Barn Party Menu

Swanson Vineyards

Swanson Pinot Grigio
Swanson Merlot
Swanson Angelica

Smoked Salmon with Lemon Zest and Dill on Crostini with Crème Fraîche

Creole Tomato Soup with Green Onion and Sour Cream*

Stuffed Pork Tenderloin with Sweet Potatoes*

Fig Tart with Almond Mascarpone*

Swanson Vineyards
1050 Oakville Crossroads
P.O. Box 148
Oakville, CA 94562
Telephone: 707.944.0905
www.swansonvineyards.com
Swanson Vineyard Salon
Telephone: 707.967.3500

Elizabeth and Clarke Swanson, proprietors of Swanson Vineyards, live on an old-fashioned vineyard nestled in Napa Valley. They enjoy creating "Entertaining Magic" for their friends and family. Terry Sweetland is "Le Cook" at the Swanson's, she is a part of their family and she has "soul". She can create Cuban, New Orleans, Italian... and adores using the abundant vegetables and fruits from the garden in preparing fabulous dinners!

CREOLE TOMATO SOUP

Ingredients:
1/4 cup butter
1 cup onion, chopped
3 large tomatoes
4 tablespoons butter
1/4 cup heavy cream
Salt and pepper, to taste
1/2 cup chives, chopped
1 pint sour cream

Preparation:
Sauté butter and onion and cook for 2 to 3 minutes. Set aside. Roast tomatoes in 4 tablespoons of butter for approximately 10 minutes at 400 degrees or until you can peel easily. Peel tomatoes and add them to the onion and butter mixture. Cook 2 to 3 minutes, then put mixture in a blender and mix on medium for 1 minute. Add 1/4 cup cream and salt and pepper. Mix until blended and pour into soup bowls. Garnish with a dollop of sour cream and chopped chives. Serve at room temperature.

STUFFED PORK TENDERLOIN

Ingredients:
16 to 20 ounce pork filet butterflied
10 to 12 cloves garlic, peeled and chopped
1/2 cup olive oil or to taste
9 ounces pre-washed spinach
4 ounces feta cheese with basil and tomatoes

Preparation:
Sauté garlic in olive oil for a few minutes. Add spinach and cook for about 5 to minutes until soft. Add the feta and heat through. Put mixture on the top of the butterflied pork filet and roll up. Secure with toothpicks. Bake at 350 degrees for 30 to 35 minutes. Let cool for 10 minutes and slice. Serve with sweet potatoes and swiss chard.

FIG TART WITH ALMOND MARSCARPONE

Crust Ingredients:
1 1/4 cups flour
1 stick butter
1 tablespoon ice water

Preparation:
Put all ingredients in a Cuisinart and pulse to the right consistency. Form into a ball and roll out into parchment paper so the circle is big enough for your pie shell.

Filling Ingredients:
20 fresh figs*, cut in half
1/3 cup Cuban or brown sugar
1/4 cup flour
20 small pieces of butter to put on top of the figs before baking

Preparation:
Arrange the figs, cut side up in the pie shell in a circular or fan shaped fashion making as many circles as you can. Sprinkle with sugar, flour and dot each fig with butter. Cook for about 25 minutes at 375 degrees, or until the pie crust is done.

Topping Ingredients:
1/2 pint sour cream
1/3 cup Confectioner's sugar
Almond Marscarpone, to taste

Preparation:
Mix together until smooth and top the fig tart when serving.

* You can substitute peaches or pears for figs.

Girl's Night Out Menu

Martin Wine Cellar

Chilled Chablis

Artichoke Risotto Cakes*

Marinated Grilled Vegetables*

Boudin Stuffed Cornish Hens with Tabasco® Pepper Jelly Glaze*

Coffee with Amaretto and Whipped Cream

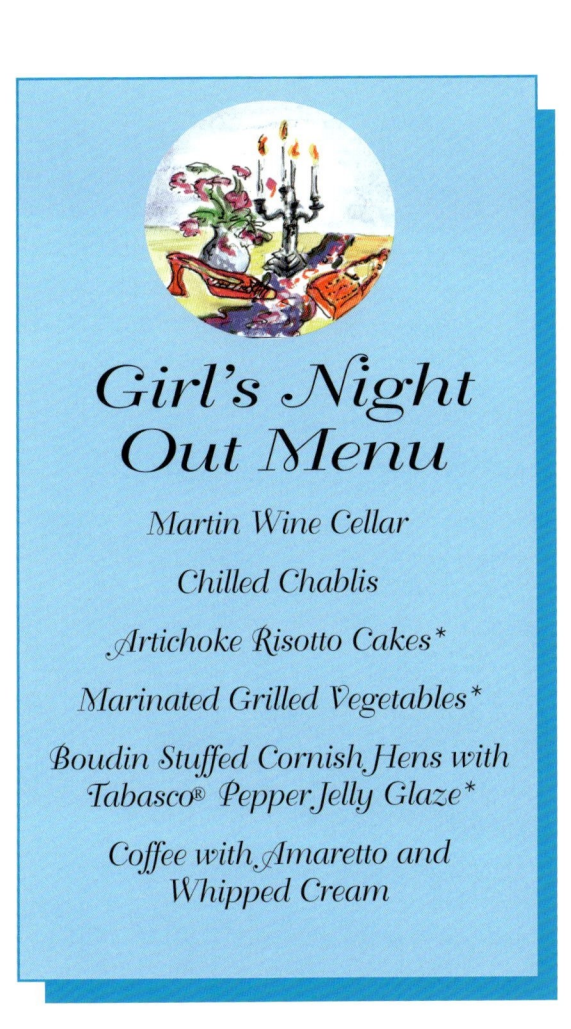

Martin Wine Cellar
3827 Baronne St
New Orleans, LA 70115
Telephone: 504.899.7411 or 800.298.4274

714 Elmeer (1200 block of Veterans Memorial Blvd)
Metairie, LA 70005
Phone 504.896.7300 or 888.407.7496

Martin Wine Cellar, New Orleans premier wine and gourmet food shop, was founded in 1946 by Dave Martin with one simple goal: to offer the finest quality products at great prices, and with exceptional service. Today this philosophy still holds true. Martin Wine Cellar has one of the largest selections of fine wine in the South and acknowledged experts who can help select the perfect bottle for any occasion. Locals flock to Martin's upscale deli for savory sandwiches, delectable salads and creative daily lunch specials. Martin's culinary team is capable of catering any event from 2 to 2,000. In addition, Martin's boasts an incredible array of cheeses, fresh pate and caviar, smoked salmon and other epicurean delights. With gourmet gifts and goodies galore, Martin Wine Cellar is a true palate pleasing paradise.

Boudin Stuffed Cornish Hens

Ingredients:
1 pound boudin sausage
1 cup onion, diced
1/2 cup green pepper, diced
1/2 cup red pepper, diced
1/2 cup celery, diced
1 teaspoon garlic, minced
1 tablespoon olive oil
1/4 teaspoon cayenne pepper
1 teaspoon dried thyme
2 cups Japanese breadcrumbs
2 whole egg
2 egg whites
Salt and pe[pper]
8 cornish [hens]

Prepar[ation:]
Remo[ve ...]
bowl
oliv[e ...]
bowl with [...]
crumbs and eggs a[nd ...]
   Salt and pepper the cavity then fill with the stuffing.
   Salt and pepper the outside and rub liberally with olive oil, place in a preheated 375 degrees oven and roast for 20 to 25 minutes until done. At serving time, coat hens with Tabasco® pepper jelly glaze. Serves 8.

Tabasco® Pepper Jelly Glaze

Ingredients:
1 cup chicken stock (homemade or low sodium)
1 jar Tabasco® pepper jelly
1 tablespoon shallot, minced
1/4 teaspoon garlic, minced
Salt and pepper, to taste

Preparation:
Combine all ingredients and reduce by 1/3 to desired consistency. Season with salt and pepper as needed.

Marinated Grilled Vegetables

Assorted fresh vegetables of your choice (carrots, zucchini, squash, asparagus, bell peppers, onions, beets, portobella mushrooms, eggplant, etc.). Cut larger vegetables into strips or rounds.

rice covered, after about 5 minutes. Add diced artichoke bottoms. Cook until rice has a slight crunch, but is still soft and creamy. Add Parmesan cheese and season with salt and pepper. Remove 1/4 of risotto mixture, place in food processor and pulse a few times. Return to skillet with remaining risotto and mix well. Transfer risotto to a parchment lined sheet pan and smooth out to a thickness of 1 inch. Allow to cool, then place in refrigerator to chill until firm. After risotto is cool and firm, cut cakes by using a 4-inch circle cutter. Lightly flour both sides of cake and sear in a hot, nonstick skillet. This can be done in advance and the cakes re-heated in oven. Serves 8.

Marinade Ingredients:
1/2 cup balsamic vinegar
1 1/2 cup olive oil
2 tablespoons dried basil
1 tablespoon dried oregano
1 tablespoon dried thyme
1 teaspoon cayenne pepper
1/2 teaspoon granulated garlic
1/2 teaspoon granulated onion

Preparation:
Whisk all ingredients together and reserve. Lightly coat desired cut vegetables with marinade and allow to marinate for 10 minutes before grilling. Remaining marinade can be kept for future use. Serves 8.

ARTICHOKE RISOTTO CAKES
Ingredients:
1/2 cup red onion, diced
1/2 tablespoon garlic, minced
1 1/2 cup Arborio rice
2 tablespoon olive oil
2 cups white wine
3 cups chicken stock
3/4 cup diced artichoke bottoms (canned)
1/4 cup Parmesan cheese, grated
Salt and pepper, to taste
1/4 cup flour

Preparation:
In a large skillet, sauté onions in olive oil until soft, then add garlic and cook garlic slightly. Add rice and stir to coat with olive oil mixture and toast lightly Add wine and enough stock to cover, bring to boil then lower heat to simmer. Continue to add stock as needed to keep

Polo Party Menu

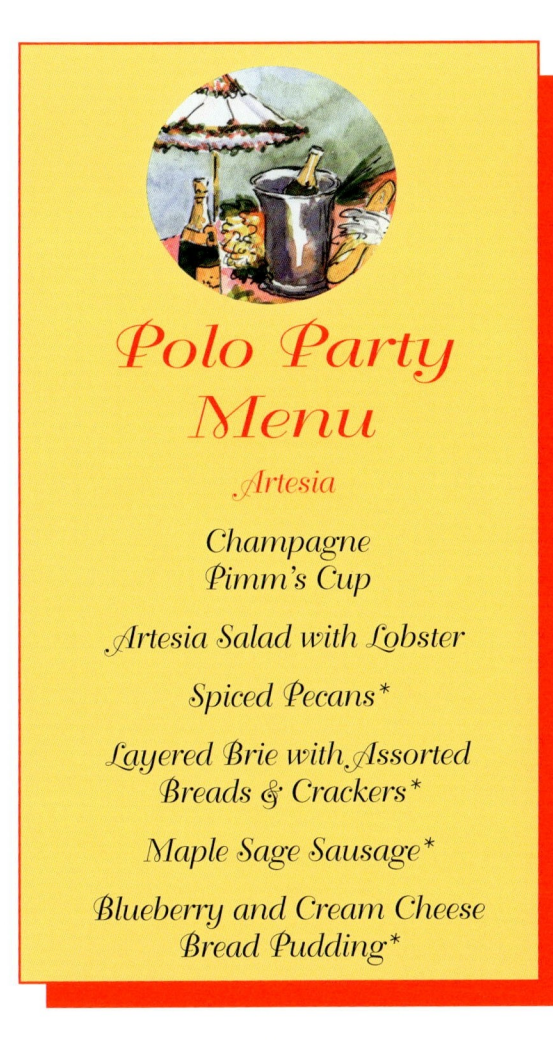

Artesia

Champagne Pimm's Cup

Artesia Salad with Lobster

Spiced Pecans*

Layered Brie with Assorted Breads & Crackers*

Maple Sage Sausage*

Blueberry and Cream Cheese Bread Pudding*

Artesia
P.O. Box 990, Abita Springs, LA 70420
21516 La. Hwy. 36, Abita Springs, LA 70420
Telephone: 985.892.1662 • 985.871.9952

The building that Artesia now occupies was built in the 1880s as the annex of the former Longbranch Hotel in the town of Abita Springs, across Lake Pontchartrain from New Orleans. In 1997, the property was purchased by New Orleans restaurateur, Vicky Bayley, who restored the exterior to its original glory and transformed the interior spaces into a fine-dining restaurant. She named it Artesia in recognition of the artesian wells that had brought fame and prosperity to the town of Abita Springs more than a hundred years before.

At Artesia, country-style informality meets urban sophistication. The dishes are imbued with fresh, natural flavors, and the ambiance is both comforting and elegant. Many of the fruits and vegetables on the menu were harvested at the peak of freshness from the restaurant's own garden. The kitchen seeks out the finest regional seafoods and meats for Artesia's guests. Artesia serves dinner and a Sunday champagne brunch. A traditional afternoon tea is also offered.

SPICED PECANS
Ingredients:
2 pounds shelled pecans
4 ounces raw sugar
4 ounces white sugar
4 ounces brown sugar
1/2 tablespoon cayenne
2 tablespoons cinnamon
3 shakes Worcestershire®
1/2 pound butter

Preparation:
Combine all ingredients. Bake at 350 degrees until sugar melts. This may be used on salads or as a garnish with a cheese board.

LAYERED BRIE
Ingredients:
1 – 2 lb. wheel of brie
1 cup sun dried tomatoes, chopped
1/2 cup black olives
1/2 cup roasted garlic
1/2 cup fresh basil, chopped

Preparation:
Cut wheel in half and take off top half. Mix above ingredients and spread over bottom half. Replace the top half and cut a wedge out and set along side to serve.

*Note: You can put brie in freezer for half an hour so it is easier to cut. Garnish top with fresh basil leaves. Serve with breads and crackers. Serves 25 to 35.

MAPLE SAGE SAUSAGE
Ingredients:
1 pound ground pork
2 tablespoons minced shallots
1/2 cup fresh sage, chopped
1 tablespoon brown sugar
2 tablespoons maple syrup (try to use pure)
Salt and pepper, to taste
3 sheets puff pastry

Preparation:
Put all ingredients except pastry into a bowl and mix thoroughly. Cut puff pastry sheets to 4-inch width. Place sausage 1-inch wide down the middle and wrap pastry around it. Place seam side down on a sheet pan lined with wax or parchment paper. Brush sausage pastry with egg wash. Bake at 400 degrees 10 to 12 minutes until pastry is golden brown. Serves 8.

BLUEBERRY AND CREAM CHEESE BREAD PUDDING

Ingredients:

1 stick of real butter
18 eggs, beaten
1 1/2 cup white sugar
1 1/2 cup brown sugar
2 tablespoons cinnamon
1 teaspoon nutmeg
1/2 gallon milk
1 pint heavy cream
1 loaf French bread [buttered and toasted]
1 pint fresh blueberries (slice some and save for garnish along with peach slices and fresh mint)
8 ounces cream cheese

Preparation:

Mix eggs, sugars, cinnamon, nutmeg, milk and cream together. Break up the French bread and layer it in a large buttered casserole dish. You can use two 9-inch by 12-inch or 15-inch pans. Pour the mixture over the bread and let stand for 5 minutes. Dot pudding with blueberries and cream cheese. Bake at 350 degrees until firm, approximately 35 minutes. When cool, slice into squares and garnish with blueberries peaches and a sprig of fresh mint.

Wild Game Dinner Menu

Bella Luna

Robust Red Wines

Fall Greens in Cranberry Vinaigrette with Roasted Pecans and Blue Cheese*

Grilled Butternut Squash Soup*

Venison Tenderloin in Beer Glaze*

Stuffed Crêpes with Apples and Caramel Sauce*

Bella Luna Restaurant
914 North Peters Street
New Orleans, Louisiana 70116
Telephone: 504.529.1583
E-Mail: info@bellalunarestaurant.com

Horst Pfeifer, a native of Germany and one of the youngest chefs ever to receive a European master chef's certificate, is Executive Chef and proprietor of Bella Luna Restaurant in New Orleans' historic French Market in the French Quarter. Since the restaurant opened in October 1991, Pfeifer has developed a sophisticated, yet eclectic, menu that includes European and regional American influences, with an emphasis on some New Orleans favorites.

In a collaborative effort with his wife Karen, Chef Pfeifer launched the Foundry in the fall of 2002. They renovated the warehouse and restored the original interior beams creating a chic versatile entertainment venue. Intimate or extravagant celebrations with the Pfeifer's are always a success.

Fall Greens in Cranberry Vinaigrette with Roasted Pecans and Blue Cheese

Caramelized Pecans Ingredients:
1/2 cup pecans
3 tablespoons powdered sugar
1/2 egg white

Preparation:
Put all ingredients in a bowl and mix thoroughly with your hands, spread on a sheet pan and bake at 375 degrees for approximately 15 minutes. When nuts appear dry, remove from oven and allow to cool.

Cranberry Vinaigrette Ingredients:
1 cup raspberry vinegar
2 cups grapeseed oil
1/3 cup dried cranberries, chopped
Salt and pepper, to taste
2 tablespoons sugar (approximately)

Preparation:
Soak the cranberries in 1/2 cup water for half an hour. Then blend the water, cranberries and remaining ingredients together. Add the sugar 1 tablespoon at a time, taste and add as needed.

Fall Greens Ingredients:
Mixed greens for 6
2 pears, sliced on a mandolin
9 tablespoons domestic gorgonzola or other blue cheese

Preparation:
Clean the greens and put in salad bowl. Add one half of the dressing and mix with your hands, taste and add more dressing if needed (remaining dressing is good for approximately 2 weeks). Place the greens on a dinner plate, sprinkle with the pecans, sliced pears and crumbled gorgonzola. Serves 6.

Grilled Butternut Squash Soup

Ingredients:
2 1/2 pounds peeled butternut squash
1 quart chicken stock
1/2 quart cream
1 cup dry sherry
1/2 cup sizably onion, diced
Salt and pepper, to taste
2 cups croutons

Preparation:
Slice the butternut squash in 1/4-inch pieces and grill until roasted. Put all ingredients, except croutons, in a 6-quart sauce pan and cook for 1 hour. Remove and pour in a blender. Blend until creamy-smooth consistency and season with salt and pepper. Garnish with croutons. Serves 6.

Venison Tenderloin in Beer Glaze

Ingredients:
1 pound venison tenderloin
Salt and pepper, to taste
Ground clove, to taste
2 tablespoons butter
Rosemary and thyme, to taste
3 garlic cloves
1 cup dark brown stock
1/2 cup beer

Preparation:
Season tenderloin with salt, pepper and ground clove. Sear meat in brown butter on all sides over medium heat, then add herbs and garlic and finish in oven for 10 minutes at 375 degrees. After 10 minutes, take the pan out of the oven, remove the venison and deglaze skillet with brown stock and beer; reduce for

5 minutes over medium heat. Strain the herbs from sauce. Slice venison on plate and lightly cover with sauce. Serves 4 to 6.

Stuffed Crêpes with Apples & Caramel Sauce

Ingredients:
8½ ounces flour
6 eggs
18 ounces milk
Pinch salt
1 tablespoon oil
2 ounces sugar
2 ounces brown butter liquid

For Crepes:
Mix all ingredients together as you would for pancake batter. Place in container and let rest for 4 hours. Heat up crepe pan or Teflon pan. Pour batter for very thin crepes. Cook until golden brown.

For Apples:
3 apples (Golden Delicious)
3 tablespoons sugar
Half a lemon
1½ cups white wine

Preparation:
Peel apples and cut into slices. Place sugar, lemon and enough wine in a saucepan to cover apples. Make sure they are covered with liquid. Cover the pot with a lid, bring to a boil, and then take the pan off the stove.

For Caramel Sauce:
1½ cups sugar
2 tablespoons water
1 cup apple juice
1/2 cup heavy cream
1 shot Calvados
2 tablespoons unsalted butter

Preparation:
Cook the sugar and water together until desired color is reached. Add apple juice and reduce. Shortly before you serve the crêpes, whisk in the cream, Calvados and butter. To serve, place 3 or 4 pieces of apple in each crêpe and fold in half. Spoon sauce over. Serve with a scoop of ice cream if desired. Serves 4 to 6.

Black & White Party Menu

Southern Hospitality Catering

Champagne

Black & White Martinis

Black & White Salad*

Black & White Zebra-Striped Bow Tie Pasta Alfredo with Gulf Shrimp*

Dark Chocolate Mousse with White Topping*

Southern Hospitality Catering
3259 Chippaewa Street
New Orleans, LA 70115
Telephone: 504.897.0477

Southern Hospitality Catering was established in 1984 by New Orleanian, John Rowland Since that time, Southern Hospitality has garnered an exceptional reputation for using the freshest ingredients and displaying extraordinary flair in presentation. Their repertoire includes major events: conventions, weddings, anniversaries... and they cater events in New Orleans and beyond from California to Maine!

Black and White Salad

Ingredients:
2 heads white Belgian endive
1 cup milk
1 (15-ounce) can hearts of palm
8 ounces canned artichoke hearts (unmarinated)
1 bulb fresh, thin, shaved fennel (Do not use green top)
16 black seedless grapes

Dressing Ingredients:
1 tablespoon Dijon mustard
1 tablespoon honey
2 tablespoons Champagne vinegar
1/2 cup vegetable oil
1 tablespoon cracked black pepper, to garnish
Salt and white pepper, to taste
Whisk to blend ingredients just before serving.

Preparation:
Soak endive leaves in 1 cup of milk for 15 minutes. Drain and place on a towel to dry. Cut leaves in half lengthwise. Drain hearts of palm and artichoke hearts. Cut into quarters lengthwise. Place cut endive, hearts of palm, artichoke hearts, shaved fennel and grapes in a salad bowl and toss lightly with dressing. Serve immediately on chilled plates and sprinkle with cracked black pepper. Serves 8.

Black and White Bowtie Pasta Alfredo with Gulf Shrimp

Ingredients:
1 stick butter (real butter, not margarine)
1/4 cup flour
4 cups heavy whipping cream
1/2 cup shredded Asiago cheese
1 tablespoon garlic, chopped
16 ounces fresh black and white striped bowtie pasta (order) or plain white bowtie pasta
2 tablespoons olive oil
2 pounds shrimp, peeled and deveined (40 to 50 count)
Cracked pepper, to taste

Preparation:
Melt stick of butter in a medium saucepan and add flour. Cook on low constantly stirring for 5 to 10 minutes. Slowly add heavy whipping cream and bring to simmer for approximately 10 minutes. Add Asiago cheese and stir. Add garlic, salt, and white pepper. Remove from heat and set aside. Boil pasta according to instructions, add olive oil, toss and set aside. In a large sauté pan, cook shrimp until done. Add alfredo sauce and toss in cooked pasta. Serve hot and sprinkle with cracked black pepper. Serves 8.

Dark Chocolate Mousse with White Topping

Ingredients:
5 ounces semi-sweet dark chocolate
1/4 cup milk, warm
1 cup whipped cream, stiff
Shaved chocolate, for garnish
1/4 cup whipped cream (topping)
1 ounce rum (optional)

Preparation:
Melt dark chocolate in a small mixing bowl over simmering water. Stir milk in melted chocolate and set aside. Let chocolate mixture cool to room temperature. Carefully fold in stiff whipped cream. Add rum. Serve in a martini glass with a dollop of fresh whipped cream. Shaved chocolate can be sprinkled on top for garnish. Serves 8.

139

Winter

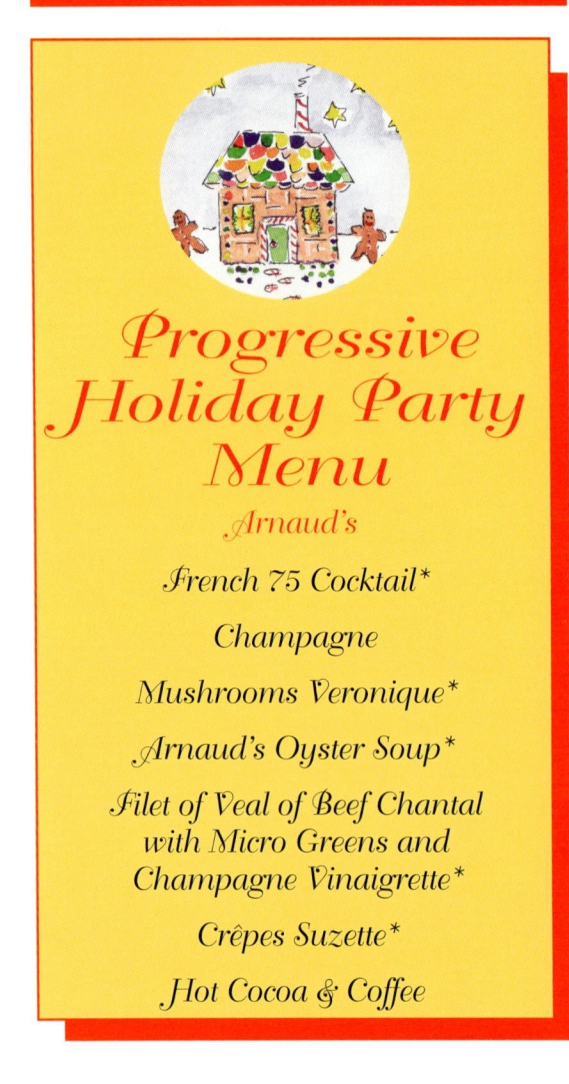

Progressive Holiday Party Menu
Arnaud's

French 75 Cocktail*

Champagne

Mushrooms Veronique*

Arnaud's Oyster Soup*

Filet of Veal of Beef Chantal
with Micro Greens and
Champagne Vinaigrette*

Crêpes Suzette*

Hot Cocoa & Coffee

Arnaud's Restaurant
813 Bienville Street
New Orleans, LA
Telephone: 504.523.5433
www.arnauds.com

Since 1918, the legendary Arnaud's Restaurant has been serving elegant classic Creole cuisine with a menu that features world-famous originals like Shrimp Arnaud, Oysters Bienville, Trout Meuniere and Filet Mignon Charlemond at lunch, dinner, or their festive Jazz Brunch. Archie and Jane Casbarian offer superb food and impeccable service in a French Quarter landmark. Arnaud's offers a cigar bar, live jazz nightly in the Jazz Bistro and the Germaine Wells Mardi Gras Museum, a showcase of Carnival gowns, costumes, memorabilia and vintage photographs.

FRENCH 75 COCKTAIL

Ingredients:
1 1/2 ounces cognac
1 teaspoon fresh lemon juice
1/4 teaspoon simple syrup (see recipe)
Champagne as needed, about 4 ounces
Twist of lemon

Preparation:
Place the cognac, lemon juice and simple syrup in a shaker filled with ice and shake only long enough to chill. Pour into a frosted champagne tulip glass, top with champagne and add a lemon twist. Serve immediately. Makes 1 cocktail.

Simple Syrup Ingredients:
2 cups sugar
1 cup of water

Preparation:
In a small saucepan, combine granulated sugar and water in a ratio of two to one (i.e., 2 cups sugar to one cup of water) and bring to a gentle simmer.

Stir and simmer until the sugar is completely dissolved, about 3 minutes. Cool to room temperature before using, and store any unused syrup in the refrigerator. It will keep almost indefinitely.

MUSHROOMS VERONIQUE

Ingredients:
60 white button or crema mushrooms, about 1 inch in diameter, stems removed (save the stems for soup, if desired)
60 white seedless grapes, washed
15 ounces Boursin au Poivre soft cheese (three 5-ounce packages), at room temperature
1 cup clarified butter, warm
2 cups Parmesan cheese, freshly grated

Preparation:
Preheat the oven to 425 degrees and line one large or two smaller baking sheet(s) with baking parchment. Brush the mushrooms gently with a soft brush or paper towels. In a large vegetable steamer set over simmering water (or a bamboo steamer set over a wok), steam the mushrooms rounded-side up for 3 minutes, to rid them of excess water. Cool.

Place the mushrooms rounded side down on a work surface and place one grape in the hollow of each cap. Scoop up about 1 1/2 teaspoons of the Boursin, and mound it over each mushroom cap, smoothing and completely enclosing the grape. Continue stuffing the remaining mushrooms. Place the Parmesan in a shallow bowl. With tongs, carefully dip each stuffed mushroom into the warm clarified butter, and then dredge gently in the Parmesan. Gently shake off any excess and reserve the remaining Parmesan for another use. Place the stuffed mushroom caps on the paper-lined baking sheet(s) and bake for 8 to 10 minutes, until golden brown. Serve at once. Makes 60.

Arnaud's Oyster Soup

Ingredients:
3 1/2 cups water
2 dozen freshly shucked oysters, drained
1/2 cup celery, chopped
1/2 cup green onions, chopped
1/2 cup onion, chopped
1 tablespoon butter, melted
1/2 teaspoon garlic, finely chopped
1/8 teaspoon dried thyme
1/8 teaspoon ground red pepper
1 bay leaf
3/4 cup whipping cream
2 cups milk
1/4 cup butter
1/2 cup all-purpose flour
1 teaspoon salt
1/4 teaspoon ground white pepper

Preparation:
Bring water to a boil in a medium saucepan. Add oysters and cook for 3 minutes. Remove oysters with a slotted spoon and reserve 3 cups liquid. Set both aside. In a Dutch oven over medium heat, cook celery, green onions and onions in 1 tablespoon butter, stirring constantly until tender. Stir in 2 1/2 cups reserved liquid, garlic, thyme, red pepper and bay leaf; bring to a boil. Stir in whipping cream, reduce heat and simmer 5 minutes. Stir in milk and return to a simmer.

Melt 1/4 cup butter in a small saucepan over low heat. Add flour, stirring until smooth. Cook 1 minute, stirring constantly, then about 3 minutes or until smooth (mixture will be very thick). Gradually add flour mixture to milk mixture, stirring with a wire whisk until blended. Add oysters, salt and white pepper. Cook until thoroughly heated. Remove from heat, discard bay leaf. Serves 4 to 6.

Note: This recipe may be prepared the day of the event, refrigerated, and then brought to temperature at the last minute before serving. Take care not to over cook.

Veal or Filet Chantale

Ingredients:
12 (3-ounce) pieces of veal tenderloin, about 1/2-inch thick or use filet mignon
Kosher or sea salt and freshly ground black pepper
4 tablespoons (1/2 stick) unsalted butter
Chantale Sauce, warmed (see recipe)
1 lemon, ends trimmed and thinly sliced, for garnish
4 sprigs flat-leaf or curly parsley, for garnish

Preparation:
Season the tenderloins on both sides with salt and pepper. Place a very large skillet (or use two skillets; avoid overcrowding at all costs) over medium-high heat and add the butter. When the foam subsides and the butter has just begun to turn brown, add the meat and sear for about two minutes on each side for medium-rare, 2 1/2 minutes per side for medium (longer cooking). Transfer two tenderloins or arrange all on a platter. cup of the Chantale Sauce over and pass the remaining sauce at the Garnish with lemon and parsley. Serves

Chantale Sauce Ingredients:
1/2 cup clarified butter
1 cup sliced mushrooms (use a mixture of shiitake, oyster, button or any mushrooms available)
1 small shallot, very finely chopped
1/3 cup dry white wine
1 1/2 cups heavy whipping cream
2 tablespoons Glacé de Viande or Veal Demi-glace*
1/2 teaspoon Kosher or sea salt
1/4 teaspoon white pepper, preferably freshly ground
1 teaspoon fresh lemon juice

Preparation:
Place a large skillet over medium heat and add the clarified butter. When it is hot, add the sliced mushrooms and sauté for 4 minutes, stirring, until tender. Add the shallot and sauté for 1 minute more. Add the wine, adjust the heat so the mixture simmers, and reduce by about half (this will take from 3 to 4 minutes). Stir in the cream, bring the mixture to a boil, and stir in the Glacé de Viande, salt, and pepper. Lower the heat and again simmer to reduce by about half, about 10 minutes. Add the lemon juice and cook for 2 minutes more. Use immediately or cool to room temperature, and refrigerate overnight. Warm gently in the top of a double boiler before serving.
*Note: Glace de Viande or Veal Demi-Glace can be purchased from www.vatelcuisine.com or a specialty grocer. (Some restaurants will

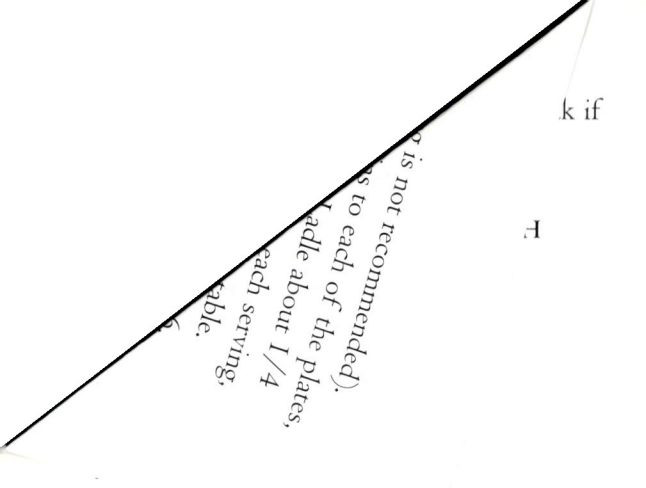

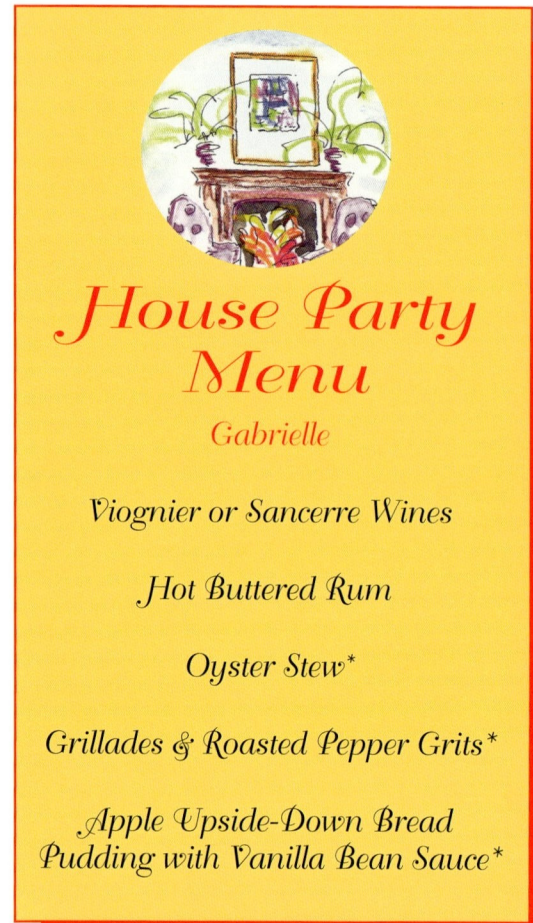

House Party Menu

Gabrielle

Viognier or Sancerre Wines

Hot Buttered Rum

Oyster Stew*

Grillades & Roasted Pepper Grits*

Apple Upside-Down Bread Pudding with Vanilla Bean Sauce*

Gabrielle Restaurant
3201 Esplanade Avenue
New Orleans, LA
Telephone: 504.948.6233

Gabrielle is a culinary gem tucked into a tiny triangular shaped building in historic Faubourg St. John in New Orleans. The owners Mary and Greg Sonnier, both chefs and spouses, dish up excellent contemporary Cajun-Creole cuisine in comfortable, cozy surroundings. The popular, petite eaterie has been recognized numerous times by national publications including Bon Appetit, Southern Living, Esquire, Travel & Leisure *and* Gourmet.

1 large sha...
8 leaves fresh basil, c...
Coarsely ground black pepper
3 cups of Micro Greens mix
   (available at fine grocery stores)

Preparation:

In a mixing bowl, whisk together the egg yolk, salt, and 1 tablespoon of the vinegar, until smooth. Whisking all the time, slowly add the oil in a thin stream. Continue to whisk until the vinaigrette thickens to the consistency of mustard. Whisk in the remaining vinegar, alternating with the oil until you have used all the specified amounts. Stir in the shallot, basil, and pepper to taste. Refrigerate for at least 2 hours, to allow the flavors to blend, and up to 2 days. Lightly dress micro greens. Serves 6.

OYSTER STEW

Ingredients:
2 tablespoons extra-virgin olive oil
3 tablespoons unsalted butter
1 cup diced tasso
1 cup diced onions
2 tablespoons flour
2 cups sliced green onion, (white part)
1 gallon oyster juice (liquor)
1 tablespoon ground fennel
2 quarts milk
4 tablespoons cracker meal
1 cup diced fried potatoes
3 dozen oysters
2 cups sliced green onion tops (green part)

Preparation:
In a 4-quart pot, add the olive oil, 2 tablespoons of the unsalted butter, and the tasso; brown thoroughly. Next, add the onions and cook them until they are clear. Add 2 tablespoons of flour, then the green onion whites, and then the oyster juice. Reduce this mixture by half. Next, add fennel to the reduced mixture, followed by the milk. Add the cracker meal to thicken and then add the potatoes. Bring to a boil and add the oysters and green onion tops. Serve immediately. Serves 8 to 10.

GRILLADES AND ROASTED RED PEPPER GRITS

Grillades Ingredients:
8 (4-ounce) veal medallions, pounded flat
2/3 cup flour
2 tablespoons salt
2 tablespoons freshly ground pepper
6 tablespoons olive oil
2 tablespoons parsley, chopped

142

1 cup carrots, julienne
1 cup celery, julienne
1 cup onions, julienne
2 teaspoons garlic, minced
3 to 4 cups veal or beef stock
4 tablespoons Worcestershire®

Preparation:
Season veal with salt and pepper and dredge in flour. In a large skillet, brown veal pieces in hot olive oil. Remove meat from pan and reserve. To the skillet add carrots, celery, onions and garlic with 1 tablespoon of the flour. Sauté for about 2 minutes then add stock and Worcestershire®. Add browned meat to liquid and cover. Simmer for 20 minutes or until liquid is thickened and meat is tender. Serve over Roasted Red Pepper Grits. Serves 8.

Roasted Red Pepper Grits Ingredients:
1 cup roasted red peppers, pureed
1 1/2 cups raw grits
1/2 cup Parmesan cheese, grated
3 tablespoons extra-virgin olive oil
Salt and pepper, to taste

Preparation:
Cook grits according to package directions. Stir in red pepper puree, Parmesan cheese and olive oil, salt and pepper to taste. Serves 8.

APPLE UPSIDE-DOWN BREAD PUDDING WITH VANILLA BEAN SAUCE PUDDING
Ingredients:
4 whole eggs
4 egg yolks
6 tablespoons sugar
1 tablespoon cinnamon
1 1/2 teaspoons ground nutmeg
2 cups heavy cream
1 1/2 cups milk (may need a little more)
1 1/2 teaspoons good quality vanilla
2 tablespoons Calvados
6 to 7 cups cubed, dry bread
2 ounces unsalted butter, cut into small cubes

Apples:
4 Granny Smith apples, peeled, cored and sliced (reserve peels and cores for sauce)
1/4 pound unsalted butter
1/2 cup packed brown sugar
6 tablespoons sugar
1 tablespoon good quality vanilla

Preparation:
Whisk together whole eggs and yolks until well blended. In a separate bowl mix together the sugar with the cinnamon and nutmeg. Slowly whisk the spiced sugar with the eggs and stir until all the sugar is dissolved. Then add the cream, milk, vanilla and Calvados; stir until well mixed. Pour the custard over the bread and soak for 1 to 2 hours.

Sauté apples in butter with brown sugar, sugar and vanilla until well combined and apples softened.
10-inch cake pan;
apples and stud with bu...
325 degrees for 90 minutes
Uncover and continue to bake a...
for about 30 minutes more. Cool sl...
then invert.

VANILLA BEAN SAUCE
Ingredients:
Apple peels and cores
1 cup sugar
2 vanilla beans (reserve some for garnish)
Toasted and spiced nuts, for garnish

Use enough water to cover apple peels Simmer ingredients together until reduced by half. Strain and reserve liquid.

To Serve:
Ladle 1 ounce of the vanilla bean sauce onto plate; top with slice of warm pudding and then whipped cream. May be garnished with toasted and spiced nuts or reserved vanilla beans. Serves 8 to 10.

Broussard's

Rose and Blanc de Blancs Champagnes
Fruits de Mer St. Jacques*
Hearts of Palm and Fresh Asparagus Bundle*
Veal Filets a la Helder with Bearnaise Sauce*
Potato Strudel*
Strawberry Sabayon*
Selection of Gourmet Chocolates

Broussard's Restaurant
819 Conti Street
New Orleans, LA 70112
Telephone: 504.581.3866
www.broussards.com

In a city that joyously celebrates fine dining as an art form, Broussard's has been a fixture in New Orleans for nearly a century. Located in the heart of New Orleans' Vieux Carré, or French Quarter, Broussard's combines a mix of old architecture, classic French Creole food and tradition to achieve an unforgettable dining experience. Broussard's first opened its doors in 1920, when an eminent local chef, Joseph Broussard, married Rosalie Borrello, and the couple started the restaurant in the Borrello family mansion built in 1834. Broussard's is currently owned and operated by award-winning Chef Gunter Preuss and his wife Evelyn.

FRUITS DE MER ST. JACQUES

Ingredients:
2 tablespoons butter
8 ounces medium or small shrimp, peeled and deveined
1/4 cup green onions, sliced
1 tablespoon garlic, chopped
1 tablespoon shallots, chopped
1/2 cup sauterne or other non-dry white wine
2 cups heavy cream
8 ounces crawfish tail meat
6 ounces lump crabmeat
2 cups sliced mushrooms
Salt, to taste
White pepper, to taste
About 3 cups mashed potatoes as garnish
3 tablespoons butter
Parmesan cheese, as garnish, to taste

Preparation:
Preheat the oven to 400 degrees. In a wide skillet, heat the butter and sauté the shrimp until half cooked. Add the green onions, garlic, and shallots, mix thoroughly, and cook another 2 to 3 minutes without browning. Add the sauterne or white wine, reduce by half, and add the heavy cream. Continue cooking over medium heat until the sauce has thickened. Add the crawfish tails, lump crabmeat, and sliced mushrooms and continue cooking only long enough for all to become well heated. Season to taste with the salt and white pepper. Hold aside warm until ready for use.

Using a pastry bag with a fluted tip, border individual baking dishes or some coquille-type shells with mashed potatoes to which you have blended the butter. Place seafood mixture in dishes, top with the Parmesan cheese, and bake in the preheated oven until hot and bubbly. Serve immediately. Serves 6.

VEAL FILETS A LA HELDER WITH BEARNAISE SAUCE

Ingredients:
1/2 medium onion, chopped
1/2 cup dry white wine
1/2 cup water
1/2 teaspoon salt
1/2 teaspoon black pepper
1/2 teaspoon crumbled dried thyme leaves
6 (7-ounce) veal filets
Salt and white pepper, to taste
2 tablespoons corn oil
4 tablespoons butter
Tomato concasse (see recipe)
1 1/2 cups Béarnaise Sauce (see recipe)

Tomato Concasse:
1 clove crushed garlic
1 dry shallots, chopped
1 green onion, chopped, white part only
1/4 cup white wine
1/2 cup chopped, skinned, seeded tomato
Salt and white pepper, to taste

Preparation:
Deglaze pan with the onion liquids. Add the butter and tomato concasse ingredients. Reduce for 5 minutes. Add the white wine and season to taste with the salt and pepper.

Preparation:
First prepare a deglazing liquid for the veal pan by combining the onion, white wine, water, salt, black pepper and thyme in a small saucepan. Bring to a boil and reduce the liquids by half. Strain and reserve the liquids; discard the onion pulp. Set aside.

Lightly season the veal filets with salt and white pepper. Sauté them in a skillet in hot oil for 4 minutes on each side until they are medium, or to your desired doneness. Remove the veal filets to a warm plate and hold in a warm oven.

To assemble, arrange each veal filet on a warm dinner plate. On one side of the veal ladle some of the Tomato Concasse, on the other side the Béarnaise Sauce. Serves 6.

Béarnaise Sauce
Ingredients:
1/2 cup white wine
2 tablespoons tarragon vinegar
1 tablespoon minced shallots
2 black peppercorns, crushed
1 tablespoon parsley, chopped
1 tablespoon tarragon, chopped
3 egg yolks
3/4 cup clarified butter

Preparation:
Cook the first 6 ingredients over direct heat until reduced by half. Strain and let cool. Then, whisking constantly in a double boiler or over hot water, add the egg yolks and cook until the mixture begins to thicken. Remove from heat while still whisking constantly. Add the clarified butter a little at a time, whisking constantly. After all of the butter is added, adjust the seasonings. Makes 1 cup.

Potato Strudel
Ingredients:
3 cups flour
3/4 cup warm water
1 1/2 tablespoons vegetable oil
pinch salt to taste
3 pounds potatoes, boiled and skinned
1 large egg
1 1/4 pounds finely diced steamed vegetables ("brunoise" carrots, celery, onions)
1/2 cup chopped parsley
black pepper to taste
nutmeg to taste
1/2 cup melted butter

Preparation:
Make the strudel dough by combining then kneading the flour, water, oil, and a pinch of salt, and allow to stand for 30 minutes. Preheat the oven to 400 degrees.

Boil the potatoes in salted water. Mash them. Add the egg, vegetable brunoise, parsley, black pepper, and nutmeg and work into a smooth paste. Roll out the strudel dough, place on a damp towel, and spread with a layer of the potato paste. Dribble with melted butter. Roll the mixture into strudel form, brush with butter, and bake in the preheated oven for 30 minutes.

Hearts of Palm and Fresh Asparagus Bundle
Ingredients:
1 1/2 dozen trimmed fresh asparagus spears
Salted water to cover asparagus
1 1/2 cups chopped iceberg lettuce
1 1/2 cups chopped bibb lettuce
1 1/2 cups chopped radiccio
3 medium tomatoes, cut into 6 slices each
1 can hearts of palm, drained and halved lengthwise

Preparation:
Cook the asparagus in salted water. Do not over cook. Allow to chill in the refrigerator in a little of the cooking water. Combine the iceberg, bibb and radiccio lettuce and divide the mixture onto six chilled salad plates. Arrange three tomato slices on each bed of lettuce. Drain the chilled asparagus and arrange them on the lettuce beds with the halved hearts of palm. Serve the salad with your choice of dressing. Serves 6.

Strawberry Sabayon
Ingredients:
4 egg yolks
3/4 cup sugar
1/2 cup whipped cream
3/4 cup strawberry liqueur
1 cup heavy cream
Marinated Strawberries (see recipe)
Whipped cream, for garnish

Preparation:
Combine the egg yolks, sugar, and strawberry

liqueur in a steel or heat-proof bowl. Cook over moderate heat and whisk constantly until the mixture is slightly thickened. Refrigerate to cool. When the mixture is cooled, stir in the heavy cream and mix well.

To serve, spoon the Marinated Strawberries into glass dessert bowls or wine glasses and nap with the Sabayon. Garnish with a dollop of whipped cream. Serves 6.

Marinated Strawberries:
3 cups strawberries, halved
2 tablespoons sugar
1/4 cup kirsch or other cherry brandy
1 teaspoon lemon juice

Preparation:
Combine the strawberries, kirsch, sugar, and lemon juice. Transfer to a covered container and refrigerate until well chilled.

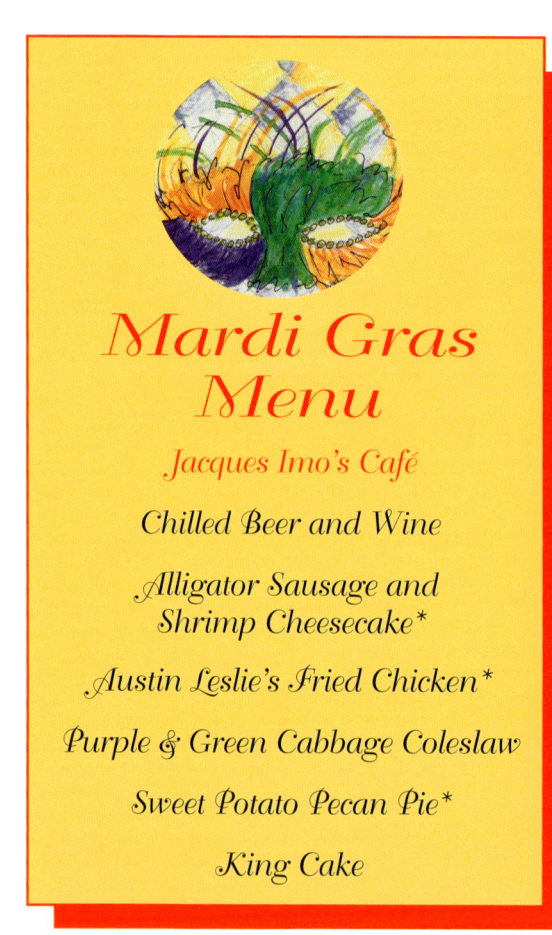

Mardi Gras Menu
Jacques Imo's Café

Chilled Beer and Wine

Alligator Sausage and Shrimp Cheesecake*

Austin Leslie's Fried Chicken*

Purple & Green Cabbage Coleslaw

Sweet Potato Pecan Pie*

King Cake

Jacques-Imo's Café
8324 Oak Street
New Orleans, LA 70118
Telephone: 504.861.0886

With $8,000 in his pocket, Jacques Leonardi, opened his restaurant, Jacques-Imo's Café, in 1996. The café, now a cozy, funky fixture of the New Orleans cuisine scene, is located in an old shotgun house in the Carrollton section of the city. The menu features Creole-Soul cuisine that captures all the spirit and spice of New Orleans. Leonardi's innovative, yet un-stuffy, approach to classic recipes has become much admired and keeps the crowds of customers coming back for more.

ALLIGATOR SAUSAGE AND SHRIMP CHEESECAKE

Ingredients:
1 1/3 cups bread crumbs
2/3 cup Parmesan cheese
4 ounces butter, melted
1 3/4 pounds cream cheese, softened
3 eggs
2/3 cup cream
1/3 cup smoked gouda cheese, grated
1 onion, medium dice
1 each green, red, yellow bell pepper, medium dice
2/3 pound alligator sausage, diced (Any good smoked sausage can be substituted.)
1 pound shrimp, peeled and diced
Pinch of salt
1/2 tablespoon Creole seasoning
1/2 tablespoon chipotle powder

Preparation:
Mix bread crumbs and cheese, add butter and press into a 10-inch spring form pan.

Bake approximately 10 minutes in a 350 degrees oven to set crust (lightly browned edges).

Mix cream cheese until smooth add eggs and mix. Add cream, gouda and mix until smooth.

Sauté onions and peppers until soft. Add seasoning and chipotle powder. Add shrimp and cook until just done. Add sausage and fold into cream cheese mixture. Wrap foil around pan to prevent leakage and fill evenly with mix. Bake in water bath (a large sheet pan) on the bottom rack in a 350 degree oven for 1 1/2 to 2 hours. Remove when an inserted knife is clean and the filling is set. Cool. Remove from springmold and cut into 12 pieces. Serves 12.

Austin Leslie's Fried Chicken

Cooking legend, Austin Leslie, is now at Pampy's Restaurant & Bar • 2005 North Broad Street New Orleans, LA 70119 • Telephone: 504.949.7970

Ingredients:
1 1/2 cups peanut oil for frying
1 (12-ounce) can evaporated milk
1 cup water
1 large egg, lightly beaten
Salt and freshly ground white pepper, to taste
3 pound chicken, rinsed, patted dry and cut into 8 pieces
1/2 cup all-purpose flour

Preparation:
In a large heavy skillet, heat oil to 350 degrees. In a bowl, whisk together the evaporated milk, water and egg. Season generously with salt and white pepper. Season the chicken with salt and white pepper. Dip each piece in the milk mixture and then in the flour. Add the chicken to the skillet and cook over moderate heat turning often, until golden and cooked through, about 25 minutes. Serves 4.

Sweet Potato Pecan Pie

Ingredients:
Dough for a 9-inch pie crust
4 cups pecan halves

Sweet Potato Layer:
2 pounds sweet potatoes, peeled, cooked until soft, cooled
1 cup brown sugar
3 large eggs
1 teaspoon ground cinnamon
1 pinch salt
1 tablespoon heavy cream
1 tablespoon vanilla extract
1/8 teaspoon ground allspice
1/8 teaspoon ground nutmeg

Preparation:
Mash potatoes until smooth. Mix in eggs, sugar, cinnamon and salt. Add the rest of the ingredients and mix to combine. Put in refrigerator to cool.

Pie Filling:
6 large eggs
2 cups corn syrup
1 cup brown sugar
4 ounces butter, melted
1/2 teaspoon vanilla extract

Preparation:
Whisk eggs until yolk and whites combine. Mix in corn syrup and sugar. Whisk in butter and vanilla.

Preparation:
Roll pie dough and line a greased 9-inch cake pan. Put in refrigerator to set. Spread potato mixture into pie shell until half full. Pour pie filling on top of sweet potato layer until almost full. Add pecans and make sure they are coated with the filling. Add rest of filling until it is topped off. Place on a sheet pan and put on the bottom rack of oven. Bake at 325 degrees until set, approximately 1 1/2 hours or when a paring knife comes clean when inserted. Makes 1 (9-inch) pie. Serves 8.

Gautreau's

Chilled Champagne and Pinot Blanc

Peppered Gulf Shrimp with Citrus Gastrique*

Turnip Cream Soup with Truffled Watercress Salad*

Grilled Salmon Roulade*

Lavish Birthday Cake

Gautreau's Restaurant
1728 Soniat Street
New Orleans, LA 70115
Telephone: 504.899.7397

Gautreau's is a popular French bistro-style restaurant favored by local patrons and visitors alike. The restaurant is located in a residential area of Uptown New Orleans, in a small building that was originally a neighborhood drug store. The antique apothecary cases now display wine and liquor selections. The dining room walls are filled with archival photographs of the city of New Orleans from the New Orleans Historical Society. The ceiling is the original embossed tin circa 1900. Gautreau's offers Modern French and contemporary Louisiana fare using only the freshest ingredients. The menu changes about every six weeks.

Peppered Gulf Shrimp with a Citrus Gastrique

Ingredients:
16 jumbo Gulf shrimp, peeled and deveined, heads left on
3 tablespoons canola oil
Pepper Mix (see recipe)
Gastrique (see recipe)

Garnish:
4 whole oranges, peeled with a knife, segments removed
16 chervil sprigs

Preparation:
In a large mixing bowl place the shrimp, and canola oil. With one hand shake the bowl vigorously and the other hand slowly shake the pepper mix so that it evenly covers all the shrimp. In either two large sauté pans or over a hot grill place the peppered shrimp on the cooking surface, cook for 2 to 3 minutes, turn over and cook an additional 3 to 4 minutes. Ladle some Gastrique into the center of each plate. Place 3 to 4 orange segments around the pool of sauce, place a chervil sprig on top of each orange segment, and place four shrimp on each plate. Serves 4.

Gastrique Ingredients:
1 cup light corn syrup
1 cup white vinegar
1 cup of orange juice (preferably fresh squeezed)

Preparation:
Heat the vinegar, corn syrup and orange juice in a medium sauce pan. Bring to a boil, then reduce heat and cook until syrup-like consistency.

Pepper Mix Ingredients:
1 tablespoon black peppercorns
1 tablespoon white peppercorns
1 tablespoon red pepper flakes
2 tablespoon pink peppercorns
1 tablespoon toasted cumin seeds
2 tablespoon salt

Preparation:
Grind peppercorns, pepper flakes and cumin seeds in a coffee grinder until coarsely ground. Mix in salt to combine.

Turnip Cream Soup with Truffled Watercress Salad

Ingredients:
Olive oil
1 yellow onion, peeled and diced
3 cloves garlic, coarsely chopped
2 bunches of leeks, green part removed, white part washed and diced
1 gallon water

3 pounds turnips peeled, medium diced
3 bay leaves
2 cups heavy whipping cream
Salt and pepper, to taste
Sugar, to taste
3 lemons
1 bunch watercress
1 tablespoon white truffle oil

Preparation:
In a large, heavy bottomed sauce pot, heat olive oil over medium high heat, add the onions, leeks, and garlic and sauté until the vegetables are translucent, about 5 minutes. Add the turnips, water and bay leaves, bring to a boil, reduce heat to simmer and cook for 30 to 45 minutes or until the turnips are tender. Add the cream and bring back to a boil, remove from heat. In a blender puree the soup in small batches until done, season with salt, pepper, sugar and a squeeze of lemon juice, keep warm until ready to serve. When ready to serve, remove the leaves from the watercress and place into a small mixing bowl, squeeze half a lemon over and 1 tablespoon of truffle oil, season with salt and pepper. Pour soup into 4 bowls and place some of the watercress salad in the middle of the bowl and enjoy. Serves 4.

GRILLED SALMON ROULADE

2 (12 ounce) salmon filets
Zest of 2 oranges
Zest of 2 limes
Zest of 2 lemons
1/2 bunch of parsley, washed and finely chopped
3 tablespoons prepared horseradish
1 tablespoon garlic, chopped
1 tablespoon shallots, chopped
Butcher's twine
Cous Cous (see recipe)
Roasted Beet Vinaigrette (see recipe)
Watercress Garnish (see recipe)

Preparation:
In a small sauté pan, with 1 tablespoon whole butter over medium heat, sweat the garlic and shallots until soft. Pull off heat allow to cool. Meanwhile using a sharp filet knife make a slit through the center of the thin side of the salmon filet, repeat until you have cut almost, but not quite, all the way through. Carefully open up the filet. Repeat with the other filet.

In a mixing bowl put the citrus zests, chopped parsley, horseradish, garlic and shallots and carefully mix together. Spread the citrus/horseradish mix evenly over both open sides of salmon filets, then carefully roll each into a log. Using the butchers twine (cut into about 6-inch pieces) tie the salmon logs about every 3/4 inch, trimming any excess string, then cut each log into 4 equal parts.

Brush each side of salmon roulade with oil and season with salt and pepper. Grill each side of salmon for 5 to 7 minutes at medium to high heat (Remember after grilling to carefully cut and remove twine. Divide salmon amongst four plates. To serve, drizzle some of beet vinaigrette around the cous cous. Place a nice bunch of watercress garnish along side of cous cous, then lay two pieces of the salmon on top of, and to the side of, cous cous. Serve immediately. Serves 4.

COUS COUS:

2 cups of Israeli cous cous
2 tablespoons canola oil
3 cucumbers, peeled, de-seeded, very small dice
1 red onion, very small dice
1/2 bunch parsley, washed and finely chopped
Salt and pepper, to taste
1 cup of crème fraîche or sour cream seasoned with lemon juice

Preparation:
In a large sauce pot bring 1 gallon of salted water to a boil. Pour in couscous. Cover, bring to a boil. Turn heat to medium, but still boiling, and boil for 7 minutes. Strain through a small-holed colander and rinse with cold water. Toss cons cous with canola oil, cucumber, red onion, parsley and season with salt and pepper. Cover and refrigerate until ready to use. Add the crème fraîche to the cous cous and check seasoning just before serving.

Roasted Beet Vinaigrette:

3 medium beets, wrapped in foil, roasted until tender
1/2 cup cold water
1 1/2 cups canola oil
1 tablespoon Dijon mustard
1 shallot, minced
2 ounces Stolichnaya Vodka
1/2 cup Champagne vinegar or white-wine vinegar
Salt and pepper, to taste

Preparation:
Using thin latex rubber gloves, coarsely chop one of the roasted beets and chop the other two into nice small dice. In a blender purée the coarsely chopped beet and any odd pieces from the diced beets and purée with cold water until very smooth. Transfer to a mixing bowl, add Dijon, minced shallots, vodka and vinegar. Slowly whisk in oil. Season with salt and pepper. Add diced beets and cover until ready to use.

Watercress Garnish:

2 bunches of watercress, washed
1/2 lemon
2 tablespoons olive oil

Preparation:
Toss the watercress in lemon and olive oil.

Gallery Opening Gala Menu
Dooky Chase

Chardonnay and Beaujolais

Cheese Straws

Broccoli Salad with Walnuts*

Roasted Hen with Dried Fruit and Raisins Sauce*

Garlic Mashed Potatoes*

Bailey's Irish Cream Custard Cake*

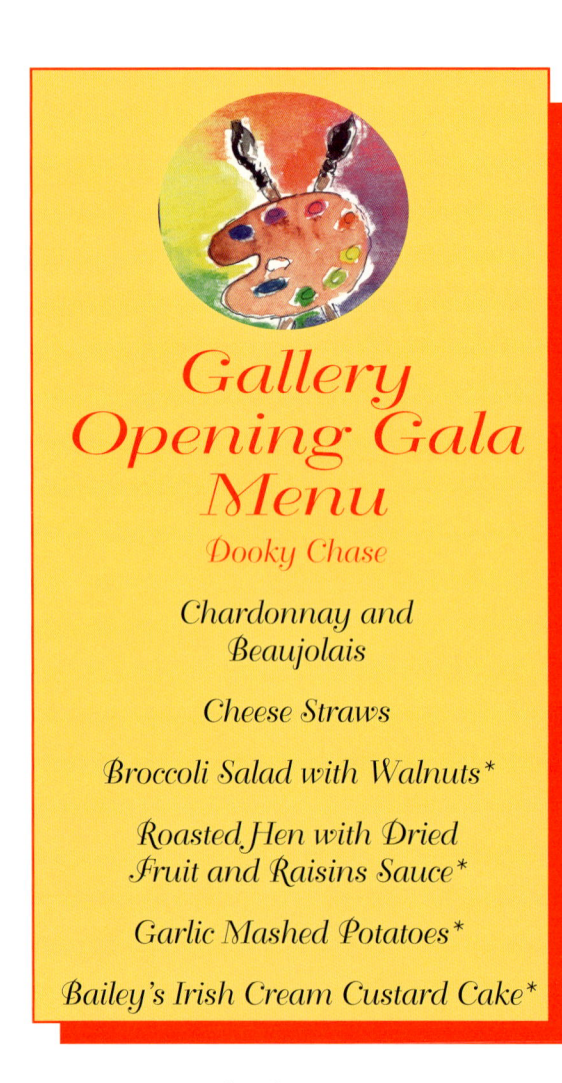

Dooky Chase's Restaurant
2301 Orleans Avenue
New Orleans, LA 70119
Telephone: 504.821.0600

Established in 1939, Dooky Chase's Restaurant is rich in tradition. The restaurant serves authentic Creole cooking, "soul food" style. Musical legends Count Basie, Duke Ellington and Lena Horne, among others, have dined there, and Ray Charles even sang about Dooky Chase's.

Leah Chase is co-owner and chef at the New Orleans' landmark restaurant. This family-run restaurant was the original creation of Dooky Chase, her father-in-law and his wife. When Leah Chase married Dooky Chase II, she was not classically trained, but she began cooking the restaurant's Creole specialties. Leah Chase has received national attention and numerous awards for her generous contributions of talent, service and time to countless organizations. She is the author of the "Dooky Chase Cookbook"

ROASTED HEN WITH DRIED FRUIT & RAISIN SAUCE

Ingredients:
1 (5 to 6 pound) hen
1/2 teaspoon ground ginger
1 tablespoon salt
1 tablespoon white pepper
1 (6-ounce) bag dried mixed fruit
1 cup chicken broth

Preparation:
Wash hen. Mix ginger, salt and pepper and rub hen inside and out with mixture. Place dried fruit in cavity of hen and tie legs together with cord. Place hen in a baking pan and pour chicken broth over hen. Roast at 450 degrees for 30 minutes. Then cover with foil and roast for about 45 to 60 minutes, until hen is brown and tender. While hen is roasting, prepare sauce.

Raisin Sauce Ingredients:
1/2 stick butter
1/4 cup onions, chopped
1 large carrot, chopped
1 tablespoon flour
2 cups chicken broth
1 cup dark raisins
Hot water
1 teaspoon ground cloves
1 egg yolk, beaten

Preparation:
Heat butter in a saucepan over medium heat and add onions and carrots. Cook until onions are lightly brown, about 5 minutes. Sprinkle flour over onion mixture and cook about 5 minutes, stirring constantly. Slowly add chicken broth. Stir well and cook about 10 minutes. Soak raisins in water for 5 minutes. Drain and add raisins to sauce. Add cloves. When hen is done, remove from oven. Add drippings to raisin sauce. Beat egg yolk slowly into raisin sauce. Serve sauce over hen. Serves 10.

GARLIC MASHED POTATOES

Ingredients:
6 medium white potatoes
Boiling salted water
6 cloves garlic, mashed and chopped
1/2 teaspoon white pepper
1 stick butter
1/2 cup milk
1/4 cup sour cream

Preparation:
Peel and quarter potatoes. Boil in water with garlic until potatoes are very soft, about 15 minutes. Drain potatoes. Place in a mixer while hot. Whip on medium speed. Add

pepper, butter, milk, and sour cream. Mix until fluffy. Serves 6.

Broccoli Salad with Walnuts

Ingredients:
2 bunches broccoli
Boiling water
1 large red onion, thinly sliced
1/2 cup walnuts, chopped
1/4 cup mayonnaise
1 tablespoon Dijon mustard
2 tablespoon balsamic vinegar

Preparation:
Cut broccoli florets from stems. Boil florets in water for 5 minutes. Remove and drain. Let cool. Toss onions with broccoli. Add walnuts, mayonnaise, mustard and vinegar. Toss well. Let chill. Serves 6.

Bailey's Irish Cream Custard Cake

Ingredients:
1 1/2 cups cake flour
1 teaspoon baking soda
1/2 teaspoon salt
3 eggs, slightly beaten
1 cup sugar
2 tablespoon Bailey's Irish Cream
1 teaspoon vanilla extract

Preparation:
Preheat oven to 350 degrees. Mix flour, baking soda and salt. Set aside. Place eggs and sugar in a mixing bowl. Beat on medium speed for about 3 minutes. Beat in Bailey's Irish Cream. Slowly add the flour mixture and vanilla. Mix until smooth. Pour into two greased 8-inch cake pans. Bake for 20 minutes. Turn out and cool on cake racks.

Custard Filling Ingredients:
2 eggs
3/4 cup sugar
2 tablespoons flour
1/2 cup brewed coffee
1/2 cup Bailey's Irish Cream
1 cup evaporated milk
1 cup pecans, chopped
2 tablespoons butter

Preparation:
In top of a double boiler, beat eggs. Add sugar and flour. Beat well. Add coffee and Bailey's Irish Cream. Mix until smooth. Add milk and mix well. Place over boiling water and cook until mixture thickens, stirring constantly, about 10 minutes. Add pecans and butter. Beat until very smooth. Let cool. Split cake layers. Spread custard between layers.

Buttercream Icing Ingredients:
1 pound confectioners' sugar
1/2 pound butter
2 tablespoons Bailey's Irish Cream

Preparation:
In a blender, mix sugar with butter. Slowly add Bailey's Irish Cream. Mix until creamy and smooth. Spread entire cake with icing. Serves 8.

Recipe Index

Appetizers
Alligator Sausage and Shrimp Cheesecake 146
Charbroiled Mussels 119
Bella Luna's Creole Crab & Crawfish Cakes with Ancho Aioli 128
Fried Green Tomato Salad Napoleon with Lump
    Crabmeat and Herb Vinaigrette Dressing 126
Fruits de Mer St. Jacques..................144
Jalapeño Shrimp with Spiced Corn Salsa..................113
Layered Brie 135
Maple Sage Sausage..................135
Mushrooms Veronique..................140
Oyster Pan Roast..................110
Peppered Gulf Shrimp with a Citrus Gastrique 148
Savory Blue Cheesecake with French Bread Rounds 117
Commander's Shrimp and Tasso with a Five Pepper Jelly Sauce ..129
Spiced Pecans..................135

Soups
Arnaud's Oyster Soup..................141
Bouillabaisse 131
Brennan's Vichyssoise Vieux Carré 128
Creole Tomato Soup with Green Onions & Sour Cream 132
Garden Gazpacho 116
Grilled Butternut Squash Soup 137
Oyster Stew Gabrielle..................142
Turnip Cream Soup with Truffeled Watercress Salad 148

Stock
Fish Stock 131

Salads and Vegetables
Black & White Salad 139
Broccoli Salad with Walnuts..................151
Fall Greens in Cranberry Vinaigrette with Roasted
    Pecans and Blue Cheese..................137
Hearts of Palm and Fresh Asparagus Bundle..................145
Lentil, Barley and Rice Salad 113
Spinach, Strawberry and Ricotta Salata Salad 123
Tomato and Onion Salad with Basil Dressing 121

Dressings
Cranberry Vinaigrette..................137
Champagne Vinaigrette 142
Herb Vinaigrette 126
Horseradish Vinaigrette..................118
Roasted Beet Vinaigrette 149

Entrees
Artichokes stuffed with Crawfish 119
Austin Leslie's Fried Chicken 147
Boudin Stuffed Cornish Hens with Tabasco® Pepper Jelly Glaze ..133
Black & White Zebra Bow Tie Pasta Alfredo with Gulf Shrimp 139
Caribbean Shrimp and Pineapple Rice..................125
Chateaubriend Marchand de Vin Champignons 130
Chicken Bonne Femme..................110
Cuban Beef with Potatoes..................125
Eggs Sardou 108
Fried Louisiana Quail with Crawfish & Corn Maque Choux 126
Filet of Veal or Beef Chantale with Micro Greens and
    Champagne Vinaigrette 141
Grillades & Roasted Pepper Grits 142
Grilled Fish with Upperline Salad Niçoise 121
Grilled Salmon Roulade..................149
Honey Gingered Barbecued Pork Chop..................123
Jerk Chicken with Fried Plantains 124
Perfect Pizza Pita Pockets 111
Roasted Hen with Dried Fruit and Raisin Sauce 150
Shrimp Cognac and Andouille Stone Ground Grits..................109
Stuffed Pork Tenderloin with Sweet Potatoes..................32
Trout Nancy..................115
Veal Fillets a la Helder with Bearnaise and Potato Strudel..................144
Venison Tenderloin in Beer Glaze 137

Side Dishes
Artichoke Risotto Cakes 134
Brabant Potatoes 116
Cous Cous 149
Garlic Mashed Potatoes 150
Marinated Grilled Vegetables 133
Mr. B's Maque Choux 123
Potato Strudel 145
Rivershack Corn Maque Choux..................127
Roasted Red Pepper Grits 143
Spiced Corn Salsa..................113

Recipe Index

BREADS
Garlic Bread 116
World Famous Organic Banana Bread 112

GLAZES
Martin's Tabasco® Pepper Jelly Glaze 133
Beer Glaze 137

SAUCES
Ancho Aioli 128
Broussard's Bearnaise 145
Brown Sauce 116
Chantale Sauce 141
Commander's Five Pepper Jelly 129
Commander's Hollandaise 108
Crystal Hot Sauce Beurre Blanc 129
Garlic Butter 116
Lemon Butter Sauce 115
Marchand de Vin Antoine's 130
Raisin Sauce 150
Roux 130
Tapenade 121

DESSERTS
Apple Upside down cake Bread Pudding with
   Vanilla Bean Sauce 143
Bailey's Irish Cream Custard Cake 151
Bete Noire with White Chocolate Drambuie Sauce 114
Black Bottom Pie 120
Blueberry and Cream Cheese Bread Pudding 136
Bread Pudding with Banana Sauce 110
Brennan's Lemon Curd Tartelette 130
Commander's Buttermilk Biscuits with Ponchatoula
   Strawberries and Sweet Cream 109
Cornmeal Pound Cake 122
Dark Chocolate Mousse with White Topping 139
Fig Tart with Almond Marscapone 132
Mississippi Mud Brownies 112
Mr. B's Lemon Pie 124
Southern Comfort Bread Pudding with Cassis Cream ... 127

Strawberries with Kirsch 131
Strawberry Sabayon 145
Stuffed Crêpes with Apples & Caramel Sauce 138
Sweet Potato Pecan Pie 147

DESSERT SAUCES
Banana Sauce 111
Caramel Sauce 138
Vanilla Bean Sauce 143
White Chocolate Drambuie Sauce 114

DRINKS
Bay Cooler Slush 117
Brandy Milk Punch 108
Cranberry Sparkle 111
French 75 Cocktail 140
Mr. Funk of New Orleans 115
Organic Peppermint Tea and Apple Juice 111

DOGGIE TREATS
Liver Pops for the Pups 120

There are so many wonderful restaurants and caterers in New Orleans that I couldn't possibly include them all. I want to thank everyone who participated and when in New Orleans I urge you to call and make reservations at these restaurants. When you try these recipes at home, get your friends together and cook all day long. Some are complex, but they are worth trying! Some recipes call for chicken, beef or shrimp stock. Refer to your favorite cookbook for these recipes or buy them from a specialty store in your area. I love to get all the ingredients and then get everyone involved creating and eating as you go!

Restaurants & Caterers & Friends:
Antoine's, Arnaud's, Artesia, Bella Luna, Kim Bremermann, Brennan's, Broussard's, Commander's Palace, Dooky Chase, Ford Reese Church, Gabrielle, Galatoire's, Gautreau's, Sallye Irvine, Jacques Imo's Café, Martin Wine Cellar, Mr. B's Bistro, Ralph's on the Park, Rivershack, Southern Hospitality Catering, Swanson Vineyards, Upperline Restaurant.

Index of Sources

Accent Annex Mardi Gras Headquarters
100 North Labarre Road
Metairie, LA 70001
Telephone: (504) 834-2003
www.accentannex.com
Mardi Gras beads, masks,
crowns, music 96

Antiques de Provence
525 St. Louis Street
New Orleans, LA 70116
Telephone: (504) 529-4342
Tables, Chairs 73

Betty Hunley Designs
6057 Magazine Street
New Orleans, LA 70118
Telephone: (504) 895-2870
Invitations, Placecards 79

Big Lots
http://www.biglots.com
Big flowers 14
Gloves 55

Dr. Bob
3027 Chartres Street
New Orleans, LA 70117
Telephone: (504-) 905-6910
http://www.drbobart.com
Be Nice or Leave Sign 49
Parasol 36
Cart 51
Chairs 93
Sign 102

Andrew Brott
1108 General Taylor Street
New Orleans, LA 70115
Telephone: (504) 239-3030
http://www.brottworks.com
Lamp & Goblets 92, 93

Ray Cole
www.raycole.com
Placemats 50
Bev's Jacket cover page ....Back Cover

Luis Colmenares – City Art Studios
555 South Galvez
New Orleans, LA 70119
Telephone: (504) 821-5243
Tent, Chandelier, Dance Floor 78
Chandelier 80
Tent Base 82
Centerpiece 93

Dick Blick Art Materials
http://www.dickblick.com
Gesso Backed Canvas 21, 29

Entertaining Celebrations/Bev Church
http://www.beverlychurch.com
See catalogue 158-159

Floral Supplies
Contact your local florist
Flower Ring 85
Oasis Ring 7, 42
Long Oasis Holder 6
Flower Pots 7, 9

Kevin Gillentine Gallery
4421 Magazine Street
New Orleans, LA 70115
Telephone: (504) 891-0509
Decoration of Tent 82
Caribbean Scene 47

Jezebel's
4610 Magazine Street
New Orleans, LA 70115
Telephone: (504) 895-7784
Faux Flowers 14

Jo-Ann Fabrics & Crafts
http://www.joann.com
Tulle 16, 18

Linens & Things
http://www.lnt.com
Faux Flowers 14

Chaffe McIlhenny
4450 Jeter Mountain Road
Hendersonville, NC 28739
www.syonic.com/glass
Wine Glasses 67, 96

Michael's – The Arts & Crafts Store
http://www.michaels.com
Frames, Foam Cut Outs,
Silk Flowers, Dragonflies 16
Flowers 20, 22

154

Index of Sources

New Orleans Custom Linens
3642 Magazine Street
New Orleans, LA 70115
Telephone: (504) 899-0604
Tablecloth, Napkins, Soaps, Glasses,
Plates 89
Candlestick 91

Orient Expressed
3905 Magazine Street
New Orleans, LA 70115
Telephone: (504) 899-3060
Linen Napkins 96, 98

Oriental Merchandise
2636 Edenborn
Metairie, LA 70002
Telephone: (504) 899-2893
Maracas 46

Oriental Trading Company, Inc
Telephone: (800) 526-9300
http://www.orientaltrading.com
Flower Boxes, Leis,
Bandana Napkins 26, 28, 65
Grass Skirts 47

Party Supply Depot
730 Martin Behrman Avenue
Metairie, LA 70005
Telephone: (504) 837-6588
White Boxes 16-17
Cake Rounds 21, 53
Cake Square 57

PetCo
http://www.petco.com
Fish Bowls 46

Pier I Imports
http://www.pier1.com
Candles 16
Market Umbrella 24, 26
Mosquito Netting 56
Banana Leaves 103

Karin Rittvo
Jackson Square, New Orleans, LA
Painting, Placemats 19
Market Umbrella 37

The Stationer
3947 Magazine Street
New Orleans, LA 70115
Telephone: (504) 895-4868
Invitation 33

Josanne Sjostrand
Jackson Square, New Orleans, LA
Market Umbrella, Painting 18

Swanson Vineyards
1000 Oakville Cross Roads
Post Office Box 148
Oakville, CA 94562
http://www.swansonvineyards.com
Alexis Wine 26-27
Notepaper, Menu Cards 87

Teri Walker
Dutch Alley Co-op
912 North Peters Street
New Orleans, LA 70116
Telephone: (504) 412-9220
http://www.dalleyinc.com
Glasses 6, 18, 20, 92, 93, 94

Index of How-To Projects

Armbands with Flowers 91
Candle Lollipops in Clay Pots 16-17
Candleholders – Flower Covered 50-51
Candlestick – Fresh Flowers in 89, 91
Centerpiece – Watermelon 44, 47
Centerpiece – Rose pavéd 76, 77
Chargers – Flowers 21
Dance Floor – Painted 78, 81
Decorated Bike Basket 48, 51
Chair sashes – Rose 23, 25
Chairback Bouquets 38-39
Chairback Ivy Sprays 69
Chairback Bouquets – Wild Grass with Greenery 75, 77
Chairback Bouquets – Pine Tree 86-87
Celebration Centerpiece with Faux Flowers 96, 99
Favor Boxes with Flowers on Top 16-17
Favors – Fern Covered Box 53, 55
Favors – Ribbon Wrapped Box 77
Flowers in Cupcakes 15, 17
Flower Photo Frames 16, 17
Flower Blanket out of Tulle 16, 17
Flower Pot Cake Invite – not pictured 17
Flowers in a Saucer 33, 35
Flower Ring with Pillar Candles 85, 87
Flowers in a Vol au Vent 88, 91
Flower Filled Shoes 104, 107
Flower Topped Cake 104, 107
Garden Gloves 55
Grass Skirts for Cocktail Tables 47
Invitation to Fish Fry 33, 35
Living Lettuce in Containers 6, 9
Market Umbrella – Painted 18, 21
Market Umbrella – Rose Adorned 24, 25

Market Umbrella – Painted 26, 29
Market Umbrella – Tassels and Fabric 70, 73
Market Umbrella Stand – Banana Leaf Arrangement 101, 103
Napkin Rings – Sunflower 12, 13
Napkin Rings 21
Napkin Rings – Watermelon 41, 43
Napkins – Bandanas Tied with Ribbon 62, 65
Napkins – Gold Stamped 96, 99
Painted Clay Pots with Sunflowers 12, 13
Painted Champagne Flutes 25
Painted Door Table 37, 39
Painted Banana Leaves 103
Place Cards – Eggs and Flowers in Pots 9
Placemats – Canvas Handpainted 29
Ribbon Roses 94, 95
Rug – Painted with Flowers 39
Service Plates – Watermelon 39
Tablecloth – Tulle 18, 21
Tablecloth – Rose Covered 23, 25
Tablecloth with Floral Border 52, 55
Tablecloth – Leaf Covered 55
Tablecloth – Flower Border 107
Table Display with Greenery and Vegetables 59, 61
Topiaries – Yew with Red Gerbera Daisies 87
Tray with Flowers and Chocolates 95
Umbrella – Decorated 104, 107
Wrapping the Wine Cart 68, 69
Wooden Box of Rye Grass with Flowers 8-9
Wreath – 4th of July 42, 43
Vases – Pepper or Gourd 61
Vases – Hanging with Flowers 67, 69
Zebra Squares 80-81

Biographies

Beverly Reese Church, one of the South's leading hostesses is co-author of *The Joys of Entertaining* and author of *Weddings Southern Style*, two best selling books published by Abbeville Press, New York. Her third book, *Entertaining Celebrations* is currently available nationwide. *Seasonal Celebrations* is the latest book published by her company, Entertaining Celebrations, LLC, which is a full service entertaining/ planning firm. She graduated from Newcomb College with a BA in American and British History and a minor in elementary education. Then began her teaching career in the public school system. She has owned and operated a flower shop in New Orleans and Mrs. Church and landscape architect, Marianne Mumford also specialize in interior and exterior Christmas decorations. She is currently the Executive Editor of *St. Charles Avenue Magazine*, has a regular monthly entertaining column, appears every Monday on New Orleans WWL-TV with an entertaining segment and is a contributor to various national publications. Mrs. Church travels extensively throughout the U.S. lecturing on all facets of entertaining and has delighted television audiences on hundreds of television programs in cities all over the United States from *Good Morning America* to *Home and Garden Television (HGTV)*.

A civic activist, sustaining member of the Junior League and a member of the Garden Club of America, Inc. she lives in New Orleans with her husband, Dr. John M. Church, Jr. and her Italian Greyhound, Sophia Loren. Check out www.beverlychurch.com for the latest tips and ideas and her show-stopping collection of centerpieces.

Cheryl Gerber has worked as a freelance photojournalist for 15 years in her native home of New Orleans. She works for several newspapers and magazines in New Orleans covering everything from breaking news to home interiors. She contributes regularly to the *Associated Press* and the *New York Times*, as well as many other national newspapers.

Chris Granger, a native of south Louisiana, has been a staff photographer for the Times-Picayune newspaper in New Orleans for about 10 years. His work also has been featured in the *America 24/7* and *Louisiana 24/7* book projects.

Sallye English Irvine is a free-lance journalist specializing in food, wine and entertaining. Her columns and articles appear regularly in several publications. She attended the Cordon Bleu Cookery School in London and has a Master's Degree in Journalism from the University of North Carolina at Chapel Hill. Mrs. Irvine is active in numerous environmental and community organizations and is a sustaining member of the Junior League. She is the creator and co-empress of Earthchic, L.L.C.(www.earthchic.com)for which she is a designer and purveyor of stylish, environmentally responsible products. She was born and raised in New Orleans and now lives in a gloriously pink Victorian house in Mobile, Alabama with her husband, four children and their pug dog. This is Mrs. Irvine's third book.

Katie Rafferty is a native of Lake Charles, Louisiana. She received a B.A. from Louisiana State University in French, studied art and art history at The Sorbonne in Paris. She then completed a year of graduate school in Aix-en-Provence. Katie moved to New Orleans, married Shawn Rafferty and has three wonderful children. She attended the Academy of Fine Arts in New Orleans for five years. She is an accomplished artist who exhibits her artwork at Cole Pratt Gallery in New Orleans.

The Celebration Collection

Make entertaining elegant yet easy, fun and affordable! Save time and money with Celebration Table Decor custom-designed by Bev Church and expertly handcrafted by metal sculptors and artists Luis Colmenares and Julia Yerkov. Create a dramatic tablespcape using The Celebration Collection, your own foliage and flowers and Bev's books: *Entertaining Celebrations* and *Seasonal Celebrations*.

Seasonal Celebrations by Beverly Reese Church with Sallye English Irvine and principle photography by Cheryl Gerber & Chris Granger.

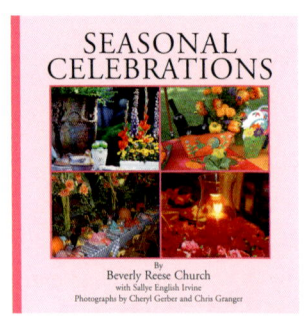

Entertaining Celebrations by Beverly Reese Church with Sallye English Irvine and photos by Tina Freeman. Month-by-month party ideas, complete with simple, but spectacular ideas for invitations, centerpieces, placecards, favors, menu and wine suggestions and recipes from New Orleans' most famous restaurants and chefs. 100 pages of ideas with 52 pages of color photos.

A. Small Palm Tree Flower Holder on page 44. Handcrafted copper and metal brushed with with tropical shades of green with one small water vial. Approximately 6" tall.

B. Celebration Single Vase on page 96. Handcrafted copper-coated steel on a square base with one large water vial. Use several of these vases filled with flowers as a centerpiece or clustered at the base of your Celebration Centerpiece. Brushed gold, silver or bottle green color finish. Approximately 10" tall.

C. Small Banana Tree Flower Holder on page 87. Handcrafted copper and metal brushed with tropical shades of green with one small water vial. Approximately 6" tall.

Celebration Centerpiece. Handcrafted centerpiece with eight large water vials. Made of copper-coated steel brushed with shades of gold paint with three gold-leafed balls at the base. Add greenery and a few flowers and you have a spectacular centerpiece. Place one in the center or two at either ends of your table or sideboard. Copper/gold finish. Approximately 38"tall.

Celebration Raised Pie Holder on pages 32 and 48. Two small water vials for flowers. Insert a round pie dish or bowl that can hold anything from Grandmother's pecan pie to your favorite dip. Gold/copper or lime green finish. About 15½" in diameter and 9" high. (Plate not included.)

Replacement Glass Water Vials Glass vials fit in these featured handcrafted Celebration pieces. Large and small vials available.

Ordering information and to see all merchandise visit www.beverlychurch.com, or call toll-free 1-888-870-7222

Celebration Large Server on pages 70 and 71. Handcrafted copper-coated steel accented by four gold-leaf balls, copper leaves adorn the base with two flower holders on each end with two large vials. Brushed gold/copper finish. Approximately 22" x 17".

Palm Frond Centerpiece on page 90. Handcrafted metal base and 5 metal tubes painted in shades of tropical green. Simply add five palm fronds and you have an instant palm tree centerpiece or add branches like maple or dogwood. Base measures 12" x 6" x 1½" and the tallest frond tube is 51".

Celebration Vicksburg Centerpiece on pages 55. Spectacular handcrafted copper-coated steel centerpiece with metal leaves and five large vases included. Open ring at the top can hold a wine bucket or a large potted plant or flower arrangement. Available in brushed gold, silver or bottle green. Approximately 52" tall.

Celebration Catering Standard Server on page 88. Handcrafted steel supported by curved legs and accented with four silver- or gold-leafed balls and with a stylish motif, this server accommodates your standard water pan, food, pan, lid and two sterno fuel holders (not included). Brushed silver or gold finish. Approximately 10" tall.

Celebration Buffet Round Server Handcrafted steel server is designed for presentation of hot or cold items! Supported by curved legs and accented with three silver or gold-leafed balls and with a stylish motif, this server accommodates your standard round water & food pans, lids and a sterno fuel holder (not included). Brushed silver or gold finish. Approximately 10" tall.

Celebration Candle Holder Centerpiece Handcrafted copper-coated steel centerpiece with three large vases included. Round disk at the top can hold a large candle (not included) or a potted plant or vase. Available in brushed gold, silver or bottle green. Approximate size 41" tall.

Celebration Chairback Holder on pages 67 and 69. Copper-coated steel with large vial can hang on the back of a chair (upper metal piece fits over the back of most chairs.) Take off the upper metal piece and use lower vase holder to hang flowers from branches in a tree or from a chandelier. Gold/copper finish. Approximate size of upper piece 6" x 9" and lower piece 13".

Lower vase holder is hanging flowers from branches in a tree.

Acknowledgements

Seasonal Celebrations has been a wonderful collaborative effort of so many talented professionals and friends.

Sallye English Irvine is an exceptional writer & friend. Her flair, colorful descriptions and style have brought this project to life.

I have worked for ten years with Chris Granger and Cheryl Gerber who are the principle photographers in Seasonal Celebrations and I am continually awed by their ability to capture the ideas presented with exceptional clarity, color and great composition.

Katie Rafferty is an incredible artist who created all of the whimsical drawings for the menu cards! What a gift she has created for us!

Special thanks to Kellie Grengs, my friend and executive assistant. She has her Masters in Costume Design from Tulane University and teaches in the Drama Department at Loyola University in New Orleans. She is multi-talented and has been an invaluable spirit and friend for the past seven years.

Sue Strachan and I have been together at St. Charles Avenue magazine for ten years. She is so intelligent, creative, fun and a very special friend! She has proof read and edited this entire book.

Lynne White has also been a wonderful giving friend; sharing her ideas, love and her beautiful home that has been a backdrop for many of the photographs shown. Tom and Carol Reese have also been generous in allowing me to photograph at their incredible home.

Thanks to Elizabeth Swanson, my oldest and best friend who created the Blowout Barn Party for this book. It was fabulous with show stopping flowers and tablesettings. It is the only party in the book I did not create and I am so grateful to her for sharing it with us.

Our chefs and restaurants in New Orleans refresh, delight and surprise us with their exceptional talent and we are known throughout the world for out cuisine. Thanks to all of them for their participation. See recipe section pages 108-151.

Thanks to Michael Ledet, PM Graphics, LLC (Ellen Verges, Robert and Phyllis O'Hair) and Garrison Digital Color, Inc., what would I do without all of you! Your expertise, attention to detail and kindness have been so appreciated.

Thanks to my family, especially my husband Johnny Church who is always supportive and loving, my children John Mark Church III and Ford Reese Church who have always encouraged me "to go for it", my mother-in-law, Kay Bailey who at age 92 is so "with it" and always gives me great ideas, my sisters Marianne Mumford, Linda Bjork and my brother Tom Reese.

Most importantly, thanks to God who continues to watch over me and my family and blesses us everyday!

I would like to thank the following for their generous help:
Rob Bjork, Gretchen Bjork, Heidi & Mark Carter, Dottie Church, Alan Mumford, Miles Mumford, Ainsley Mumford, Carol Reese, Jessica Conway, Rob Couhig, Eban Hart, Lynne & Hunter White, Clarke Swanson, Pixie & Jimmy Reiss, Jennifer St. Paul, Jasmine Chigbu, Callee Dillon, Josanne Sjostrand, Karin Rittvo, Tim Reily, Teri Walker, Andrew Brott, Judi Hill, Julia Yerkov, Luis Colmenares, The Stationer of New Orleans, Betty Hunley Designs of New Orleans, Jeannette Slakey, Kevin Gillentine, Vincent Bergeal, Dr. Bob, Laura's Table of New Orleans, Becky & Dick Currence, Mathilde and Prieur Leary, Cindy Nunez, Celia Bezou, Jennifer Rice, Charles Schroeder, Susan & Doug Johnson, Custom Linens of New Orleans, Linda & Marc Friedlander, Michael Friedlander, Brian Friedlander, Dathel & Tommy Coleman, Susan & Bill Prentiss, Archie & Jane Casbarian, Rock'n' Bowl of New Orleans, Landscape Images, Ida Rak, M.I. and Guy Scoggin, Matthew and Darcy Scoggin, and their children Guy and Mia Scoggin, Karen LaBorde, Peggy LaBorde, all my friends at Greenleaf Wholesale Florist, St. Charles Avenue Magazine, Bill & Missy Metcalf, Todd Matherne, Alan Campell & Errol Laborde, Charlee Williamson, Ralph Brennan, Patrick Singley, Cindy Brennan, Julie Brignac, Lally Brennan, Ella Brennan, Sally Graves, Vicky Bayley, Leah Chase, Terry Sweetland, Jack Leonardi, Bonnie Warren, Pip, Ted, & Jimmy Brennan, Ellen Brennan, John Rowland, Jyl Benson, David Gooch, Melvin Rodrigue, Mary & Greg Sonnier, Kim Bremermann, Jimmy & Sam Collins, Joan Clevenger, Ken Smith, Flo Braker, Jane & Archie Casbarain, Gunther & Evelyn Preuss, Horst & Karen Pfeifer, Collette Guste, Jimmy Guste and Randy Guste, Cedric Martin, Cheryl LeMoine, Jacqueline McPherson.